SET TO SEA

SET TO SEA

BY

DREW WEING

ILLUSTRATED

FANTAGRAPHICS BOOKS, SEATTLE
2010

Editor: Gary Groth
Production: Paul Baresh
Associate Publisher: Eric Reynolds
Publishers: Gary Groth & Kim Thompson

Fantagraphics Books, Inc.
7563 Lake City Way, Seattle, WA 98115.

To receive a free catalogue of fine
comics and novels, both prose and graphic,
call 1-800-657-1100 or visit our website
at Fantagraphics.com.

Distributed in the U.S. by
W.W. Norton and Company, Inc. (800-233-4830)
Distributed in Canada by
Canadian Manda Group (800-452-6642 x862)
Distributed in the UK by
Turnaround Distribution (44-020-8829-3002)
Distributed to comic book specialty stores by
Diamond Comics Distributors (800-452-6642 x215)

ISBN 978-1-60699-368-2
Second printing: June 2011
Printed in China.

For Eleanor

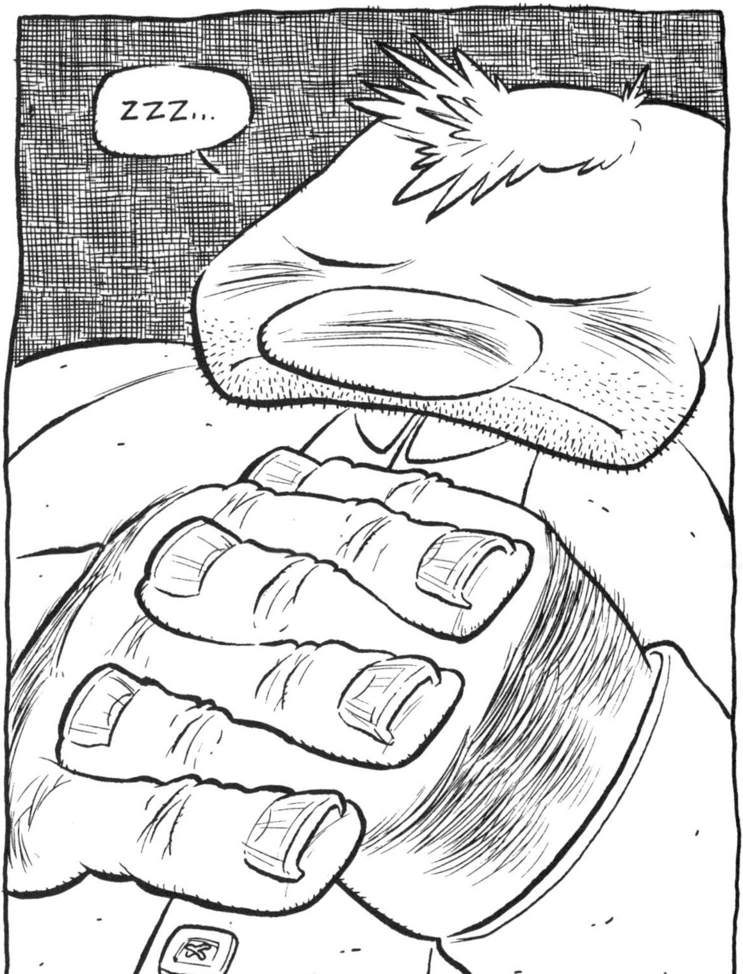
ZZZ...

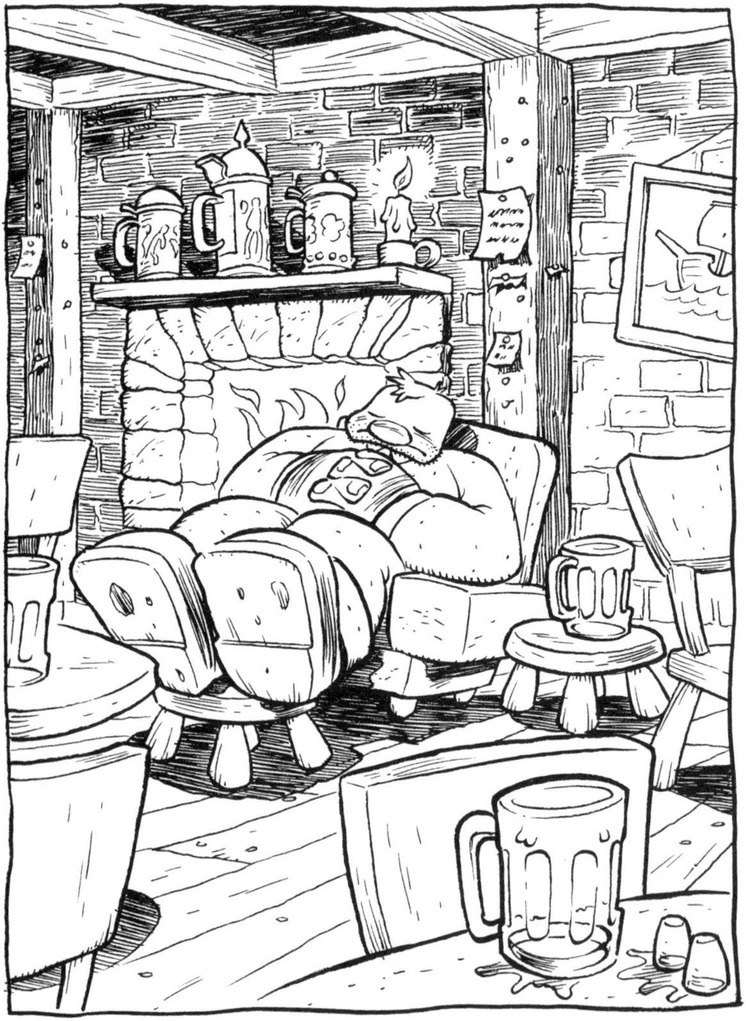

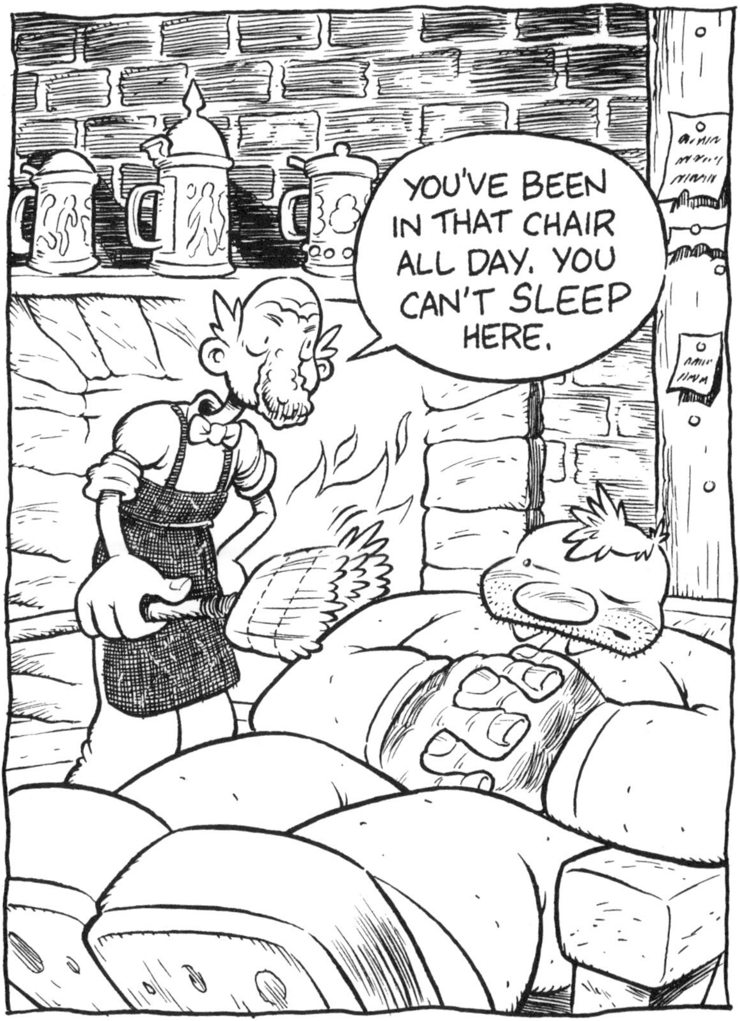
YOU'VE BEEN IN THAT CHAIR ALL DAY. YOU CAN'T SLEEP HERE.

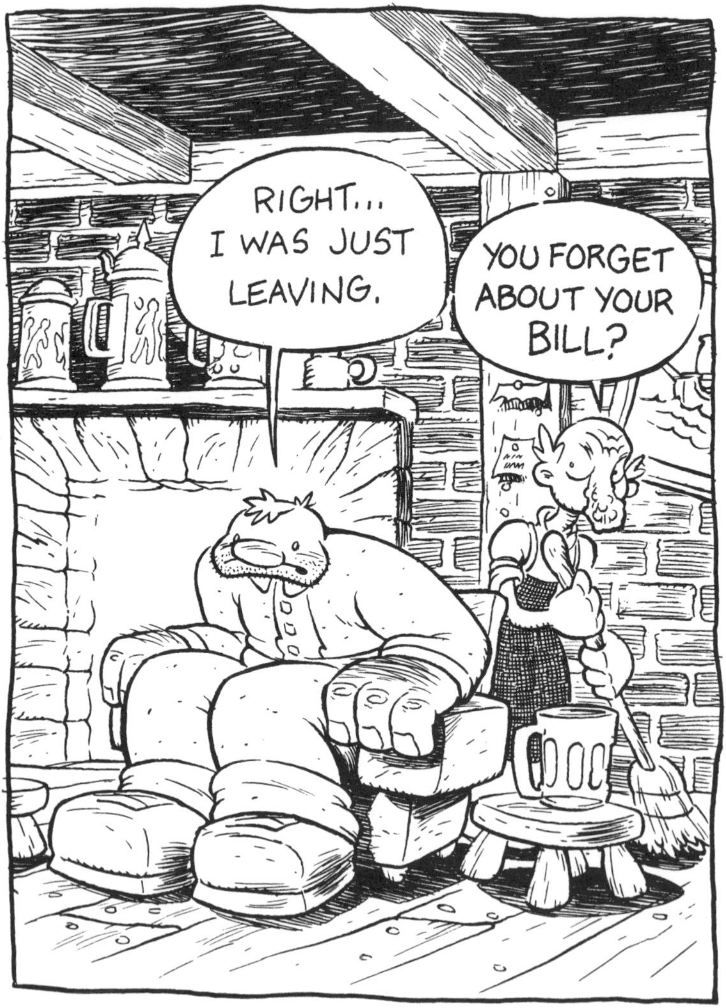
RIGHT...
I WAS JUST
LEAVING.
YOU FORGET
ABOUT YOUR
BILL?

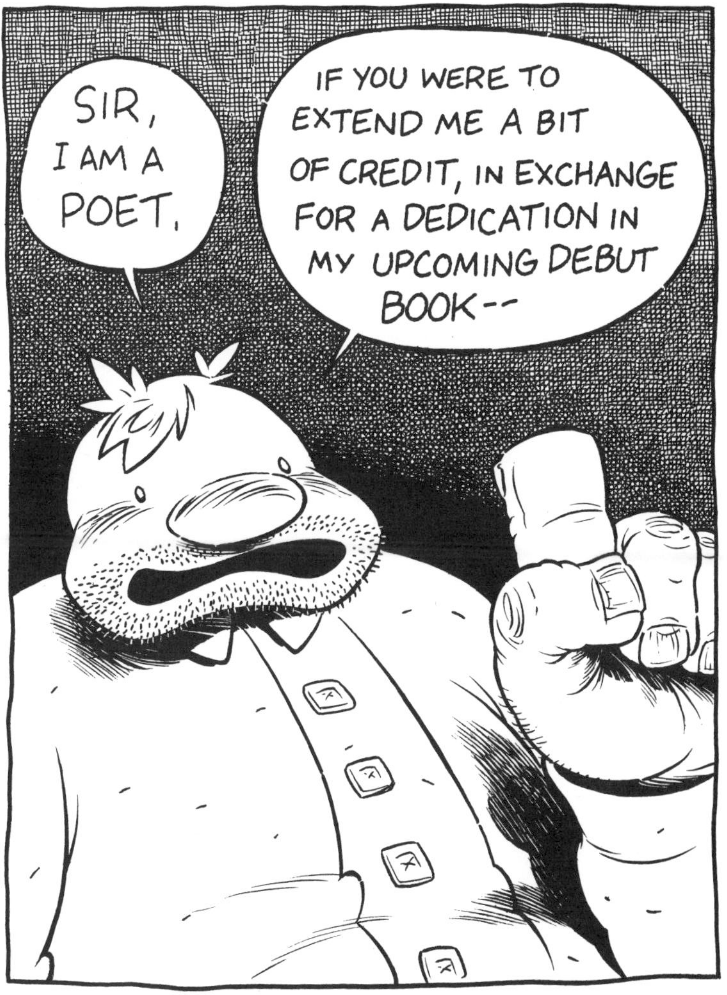
SIR, I AM A POET.
IF YOU WERE TO EXTEND ME A BIT OF CREDIT, IN EXCHANGE FOR A DEDICATION IN MY UPCOMING DEBUT BOOK--

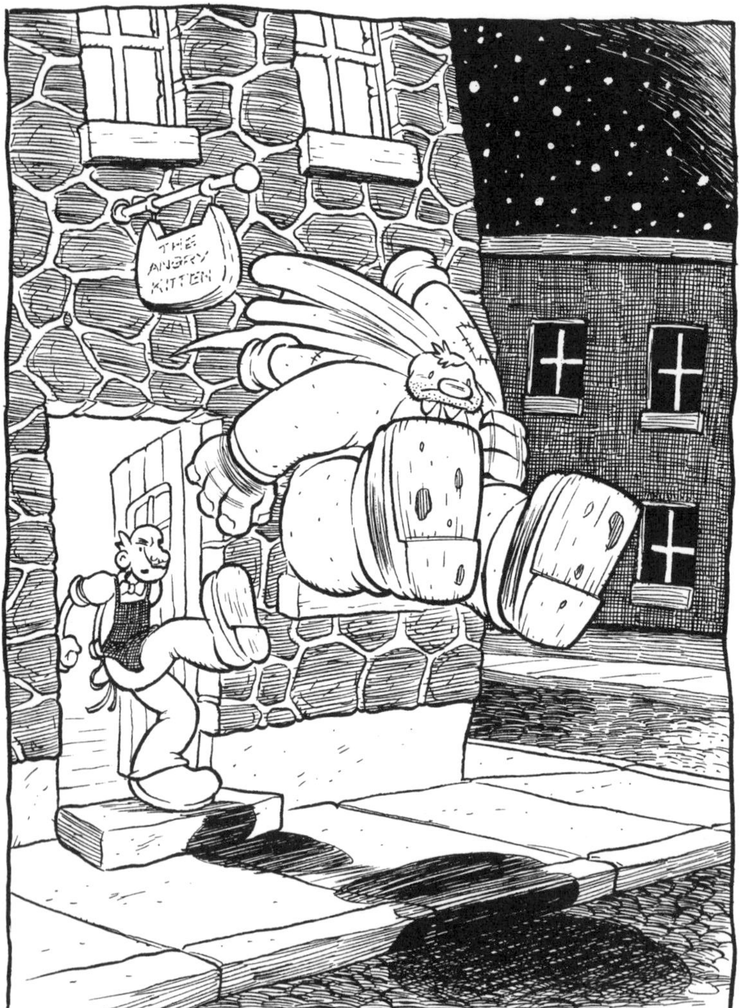
THE ANGRY KITTEN

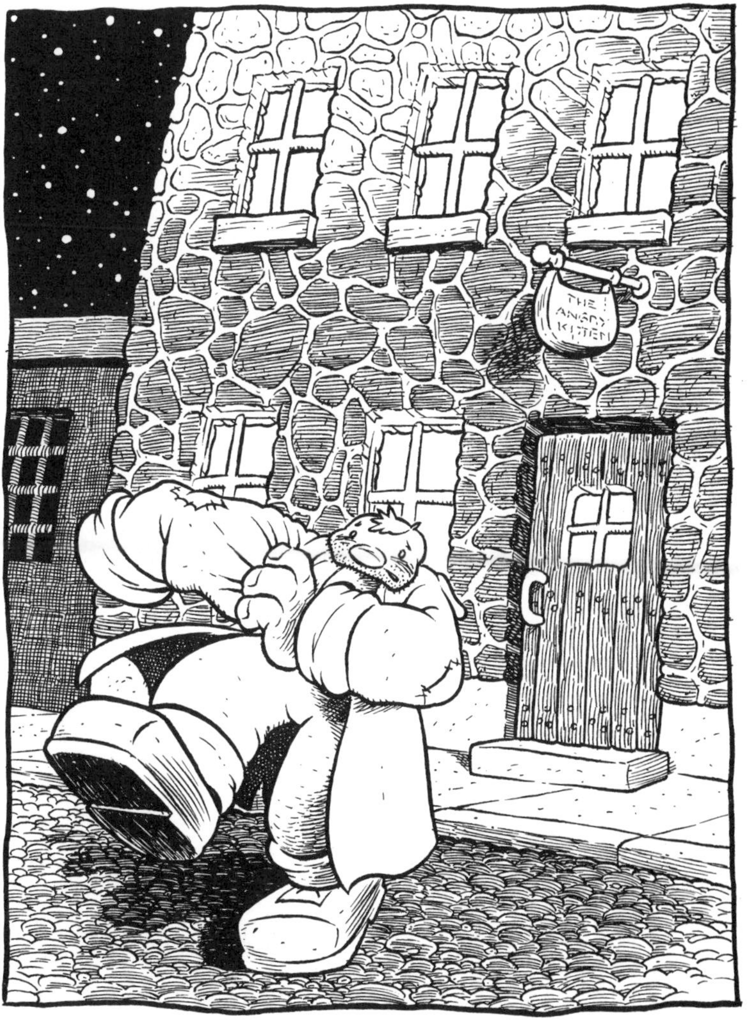
THE ANGRY KITTEN

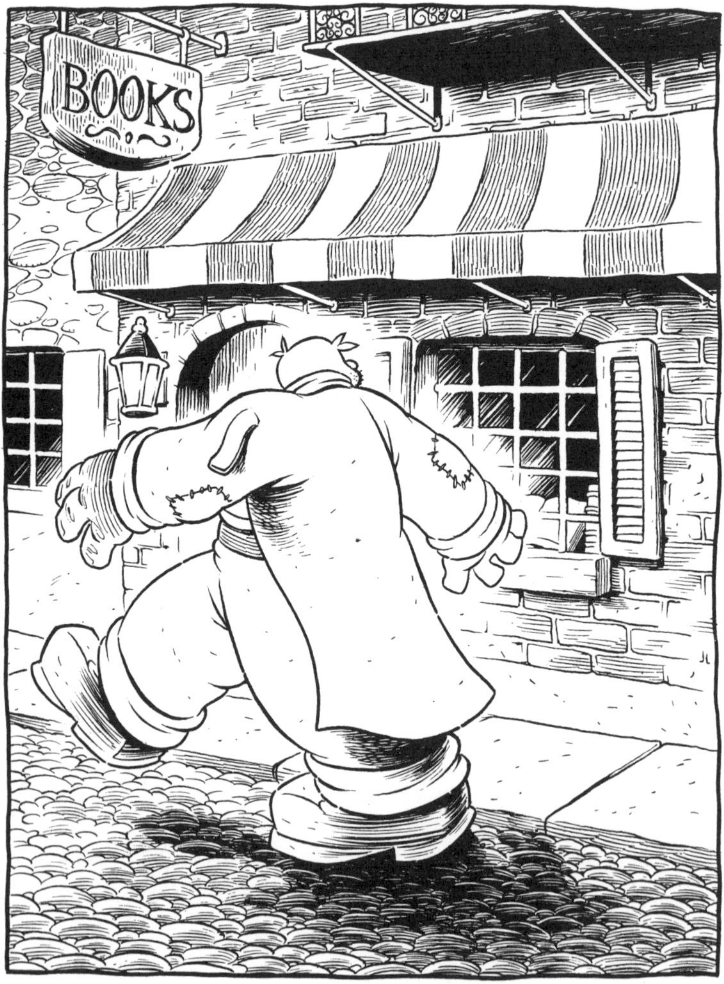
BOOKS

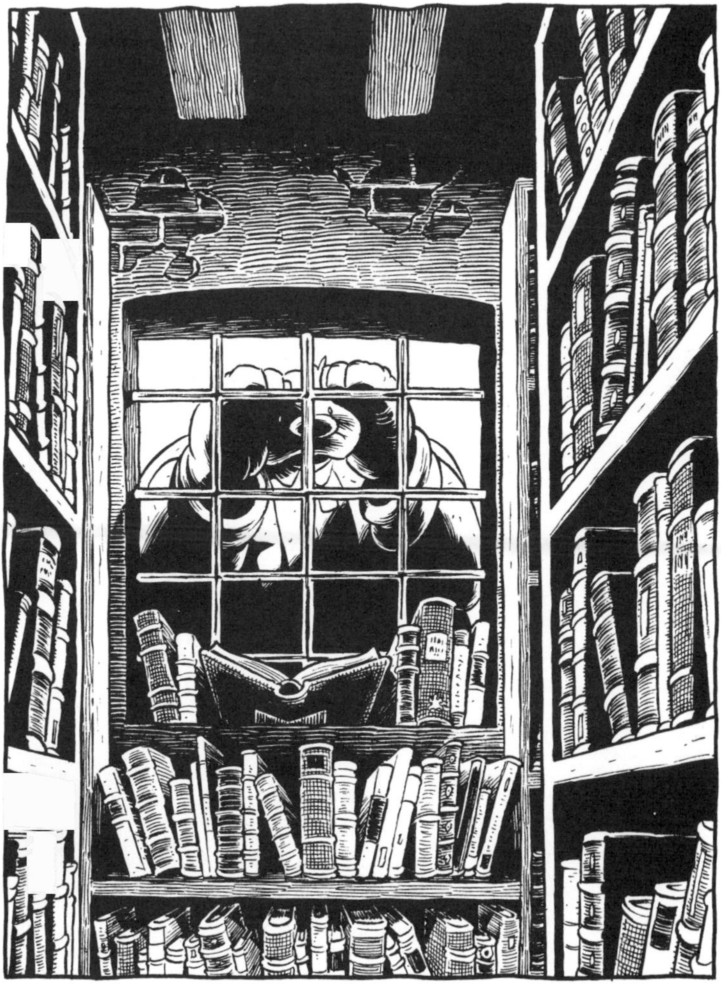

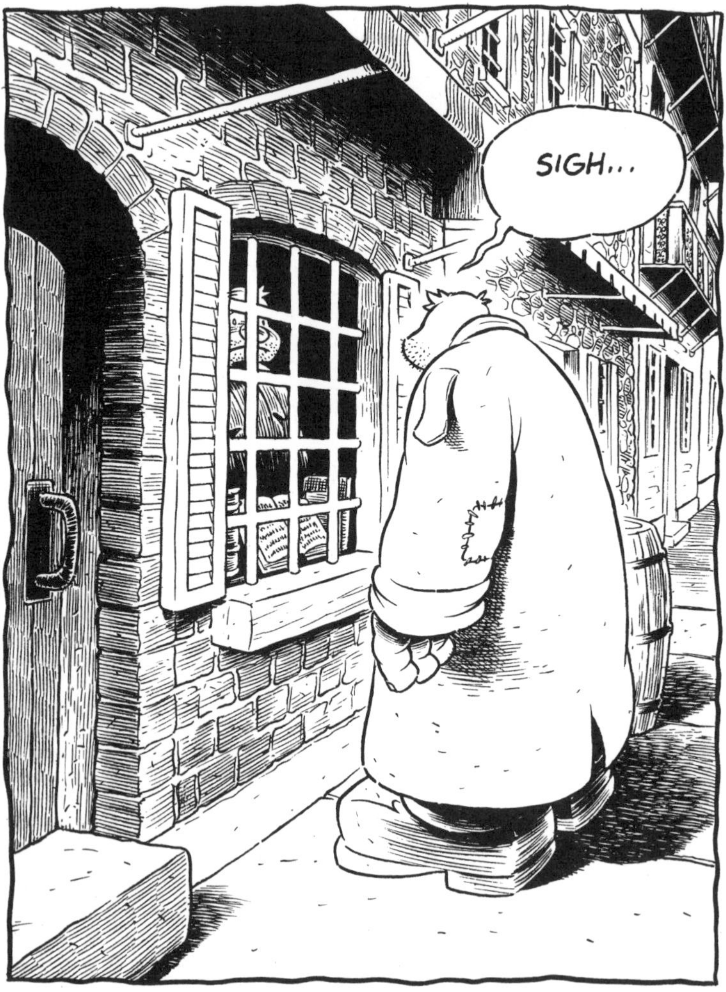
SIGH...

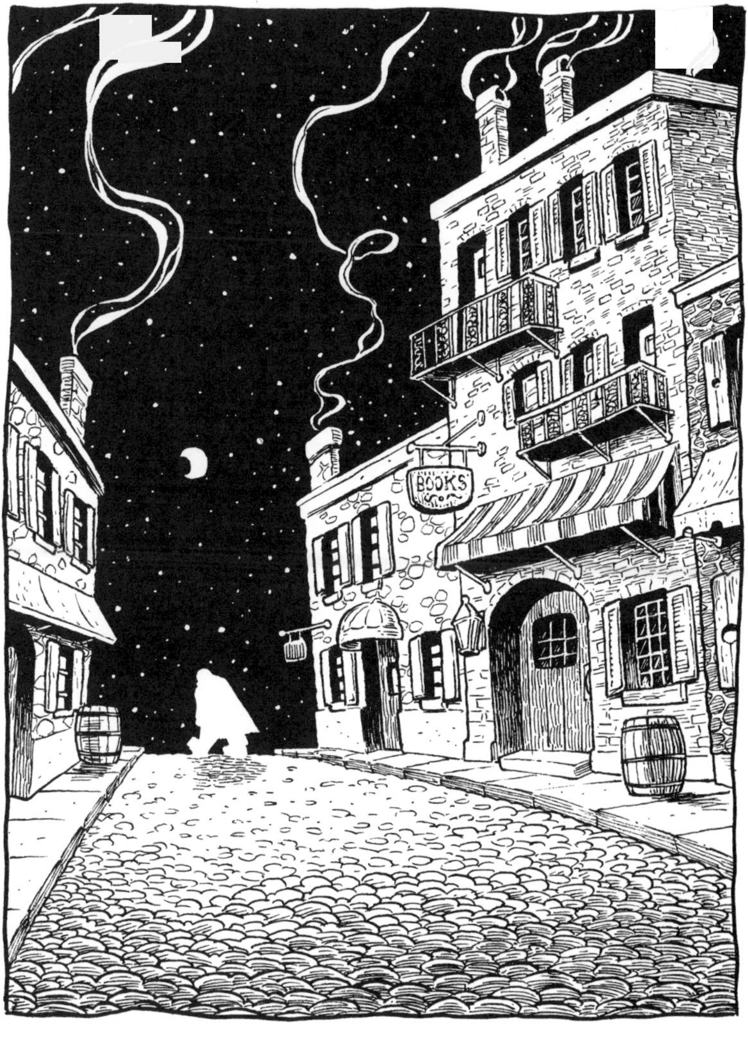
BOOKS

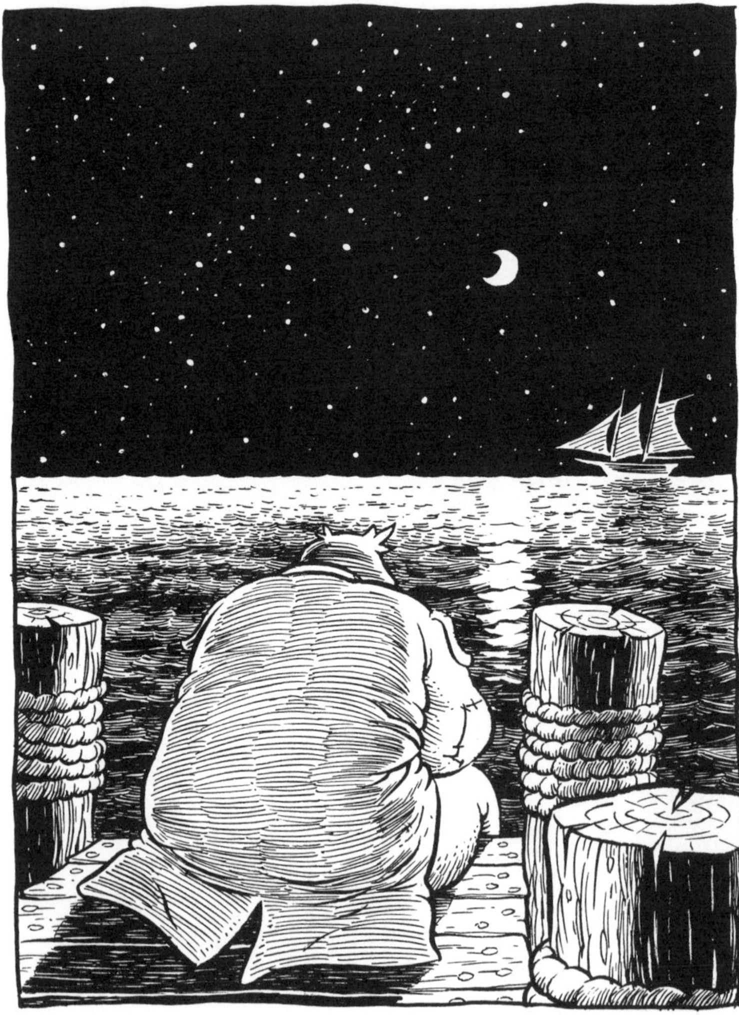

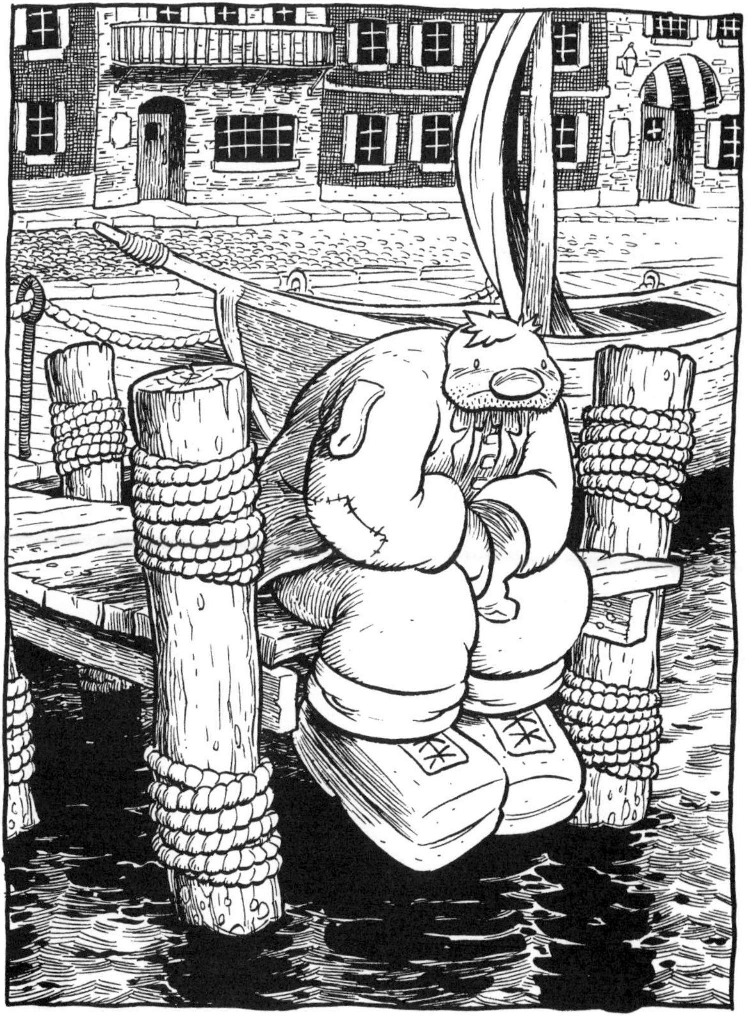

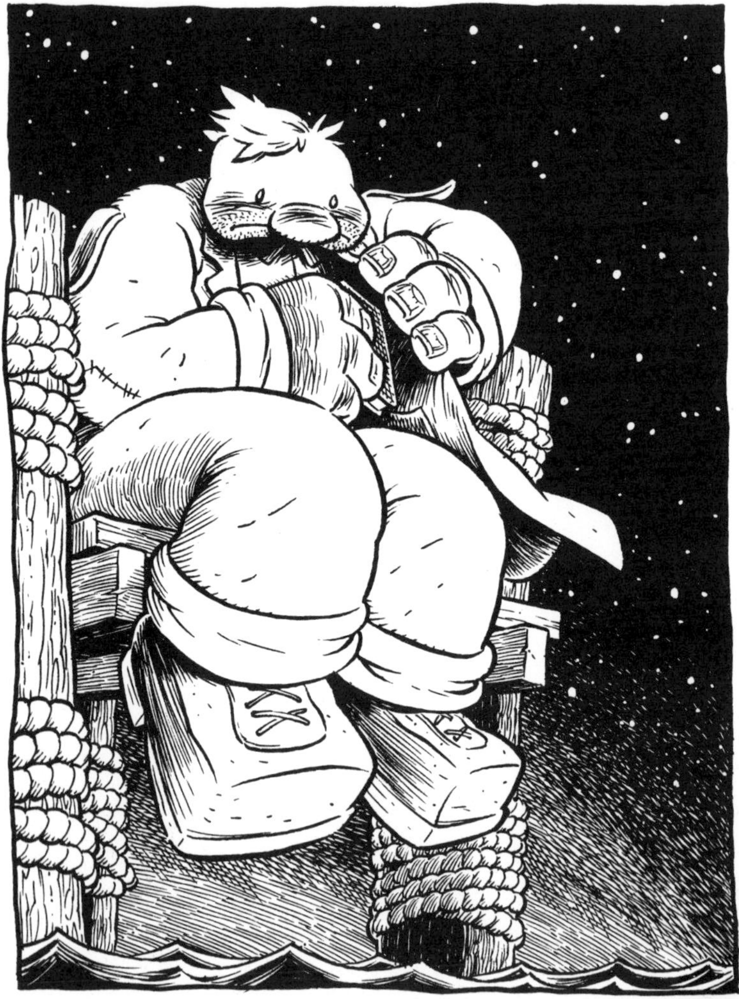

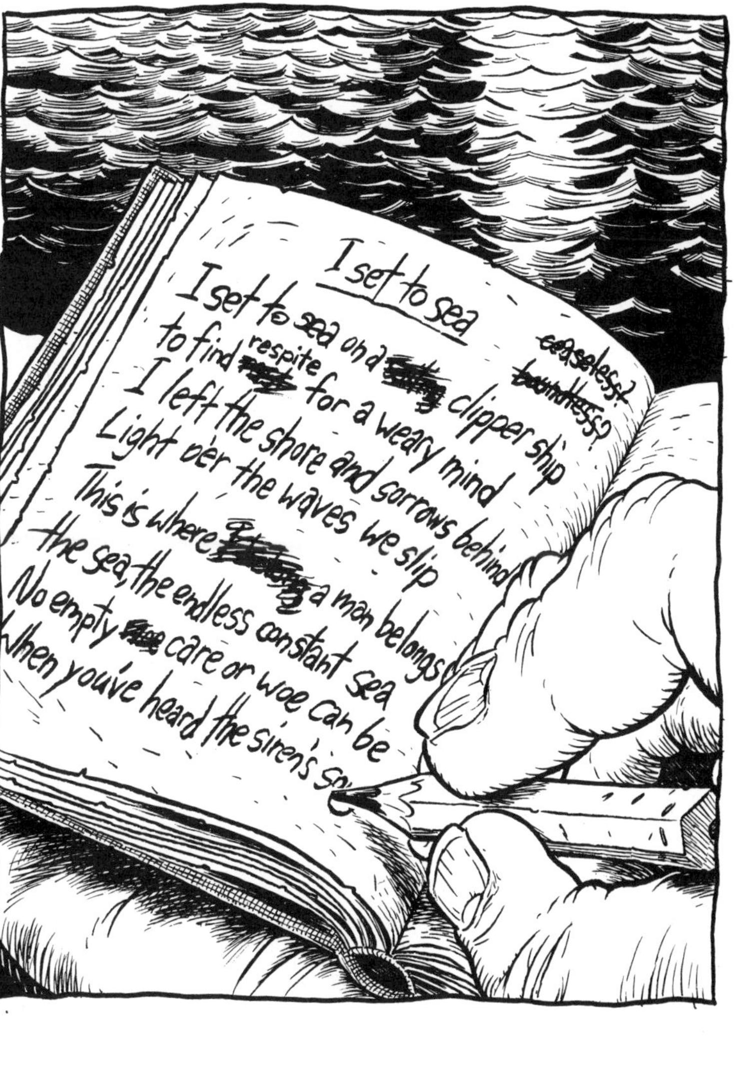
I set to sea
I set to sea on a clipper ship
to find respite for a weary mind
I left the shore and sorrows behind
Light o'er the waves we slip
This is where a man belongs
the sea, the endless constant sea
No empty care or woe can be
When you've heard the siren's s
ceaseless?
boundless?

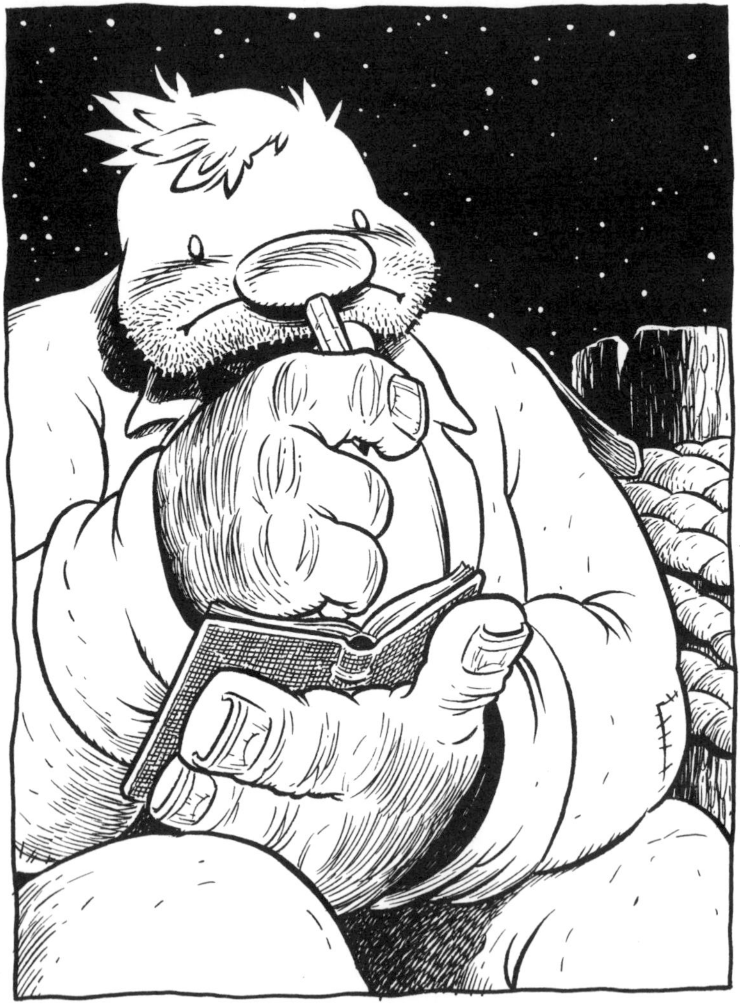

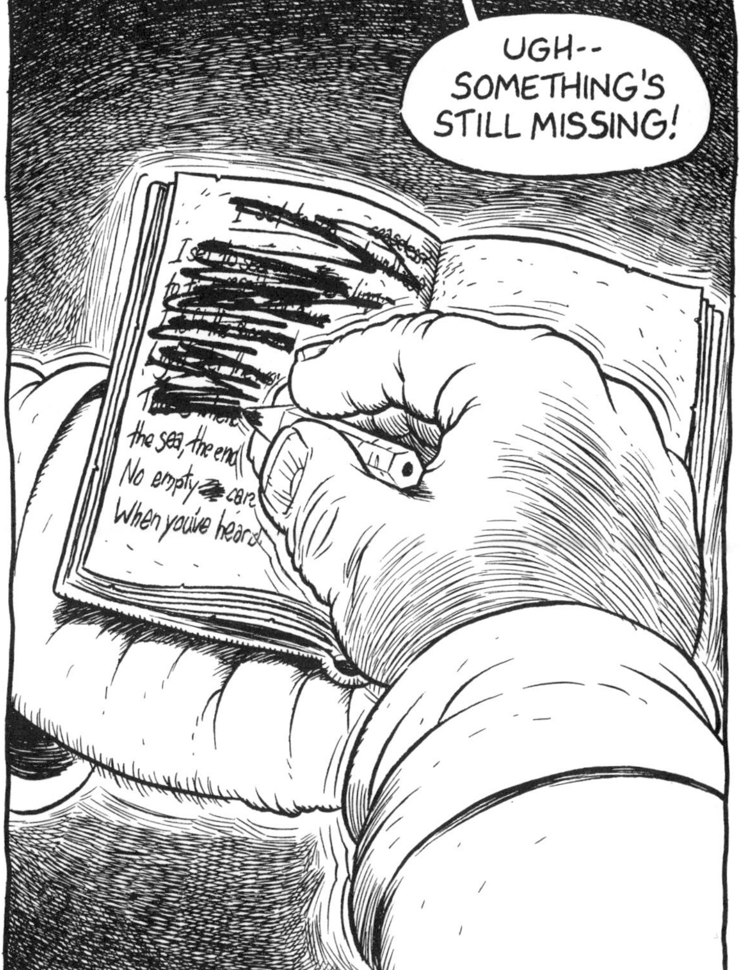
UGH--
SOMETHING'S
STILL MISSING!
the sea, the end
No empty care
When you've heard

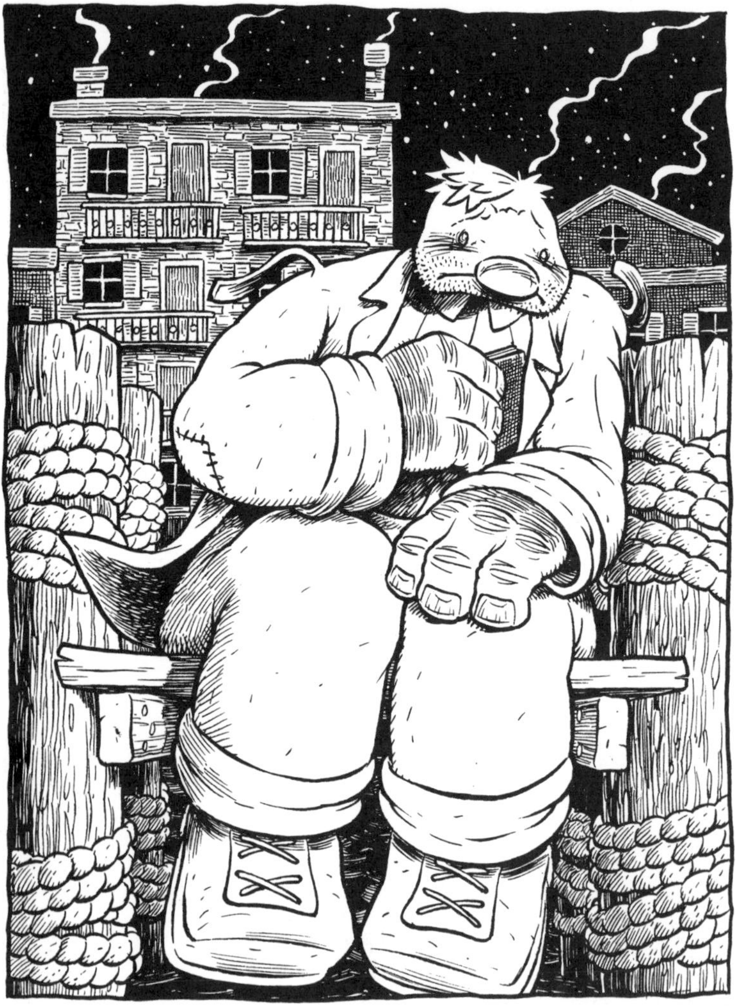

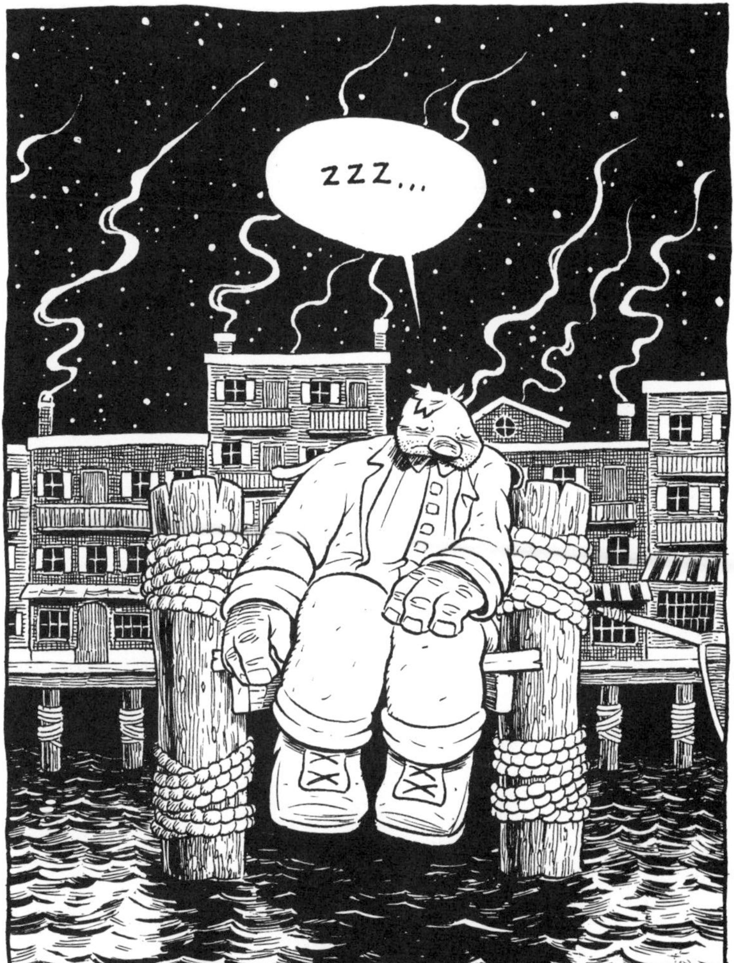
ZZZ...

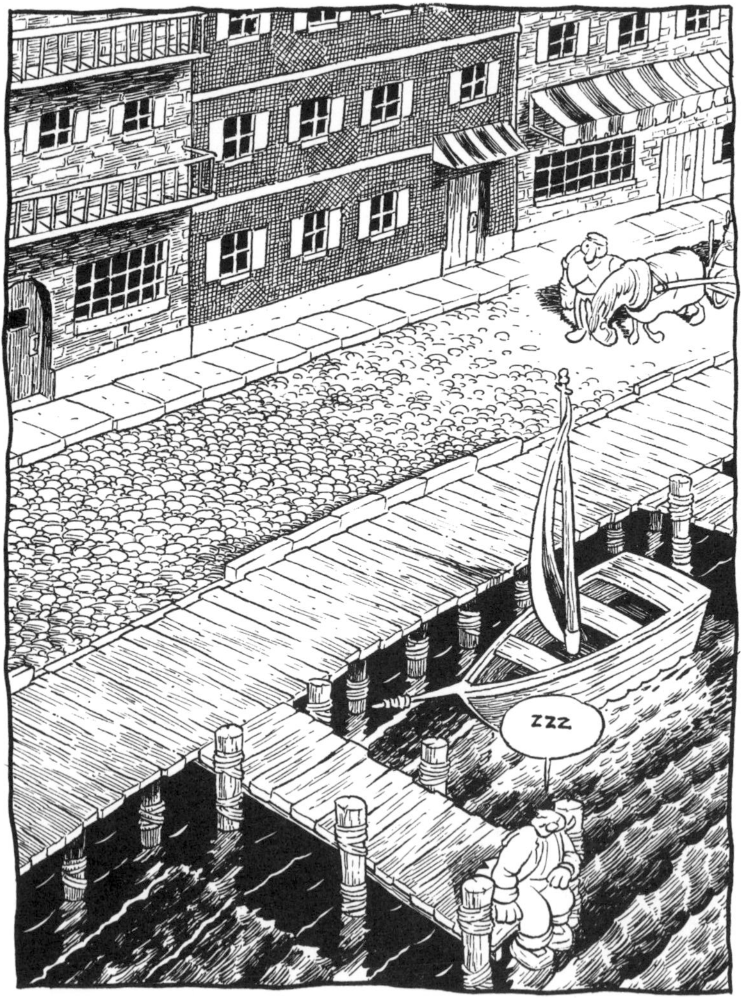
ZZZ

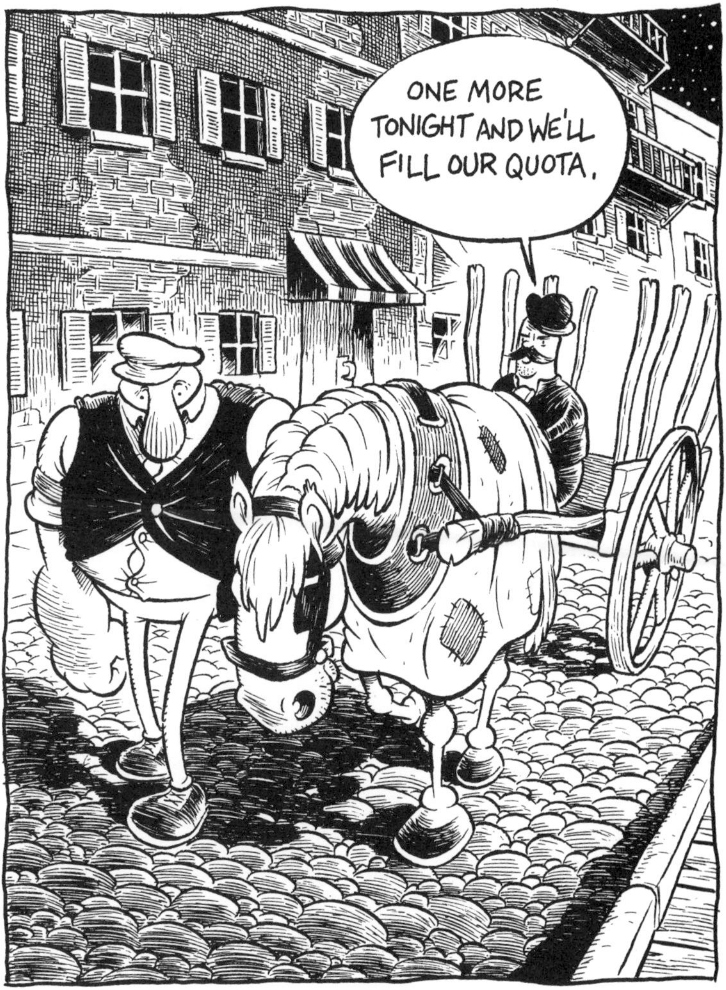
ONE MORE TONIGHT AND WE'LL FILL OUR QUOTA.

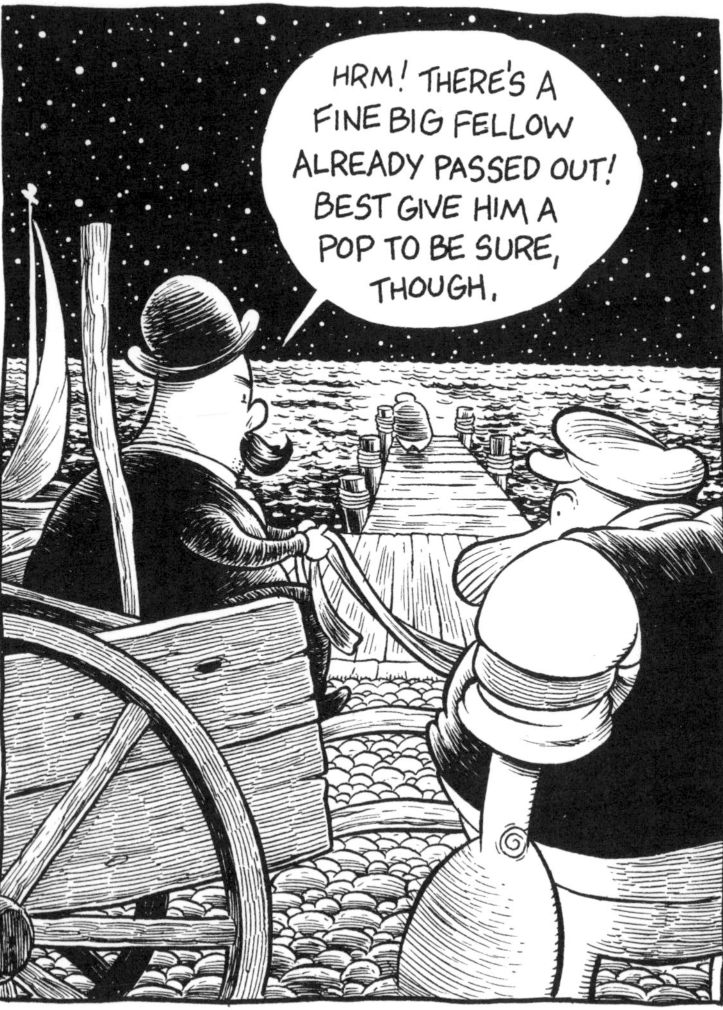
HRM! THERE'S A FINE BIG FELLOW ALREADY PASSED OUT! BEST GIVE HIM A POP TO BE SURE, THOUGH.

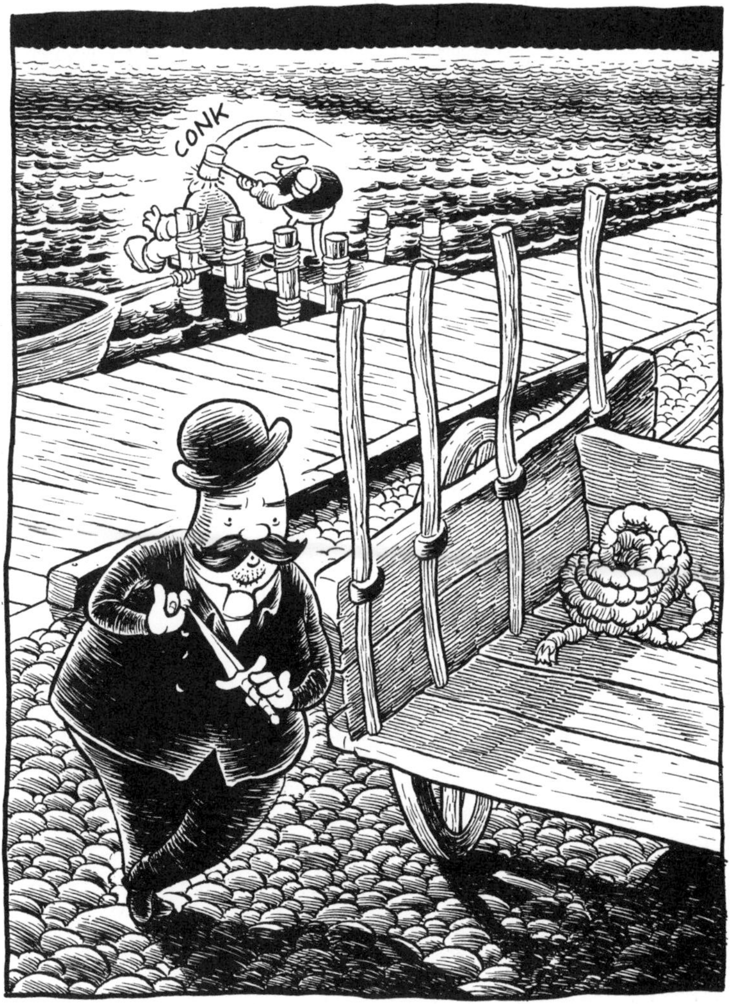
CONK

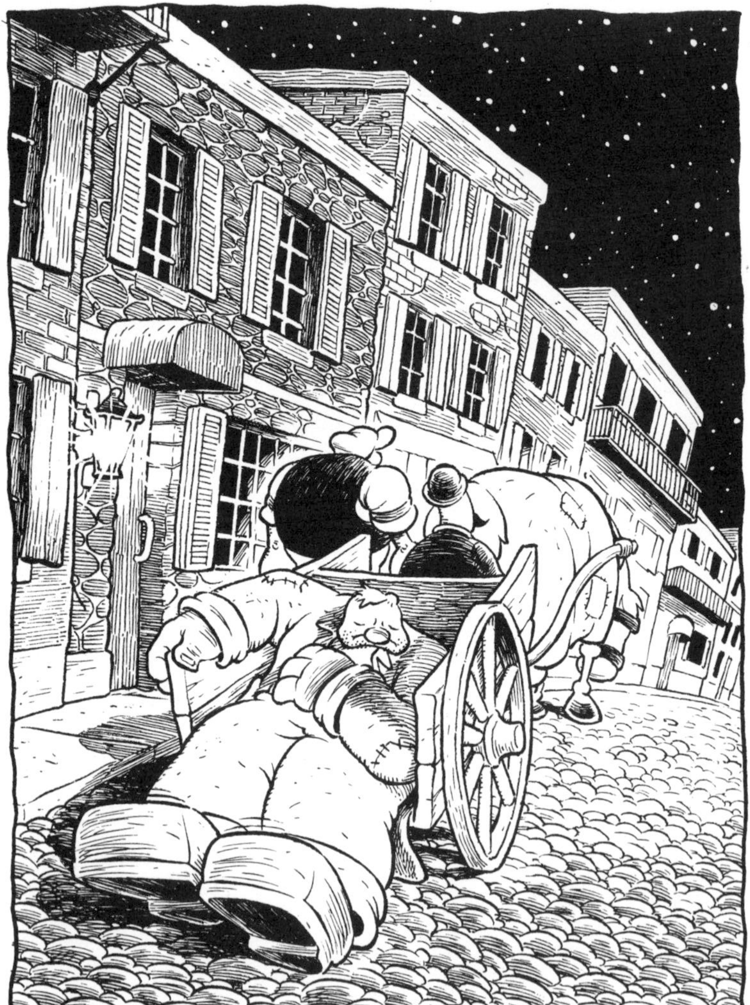

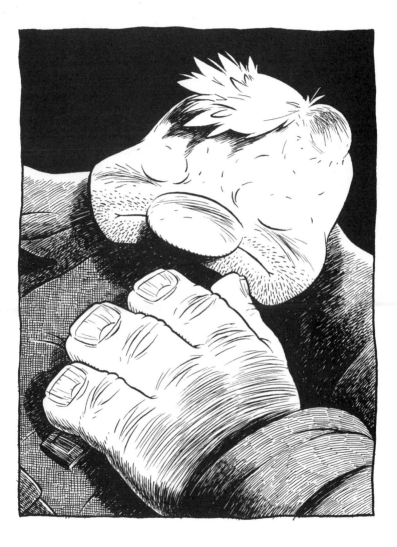

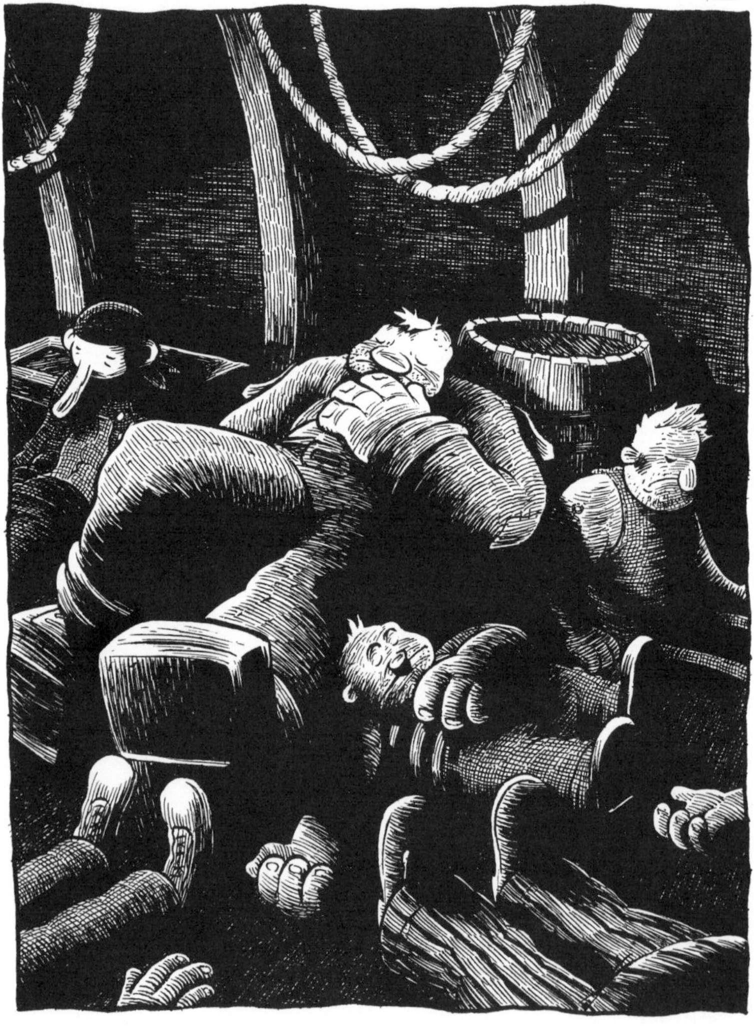

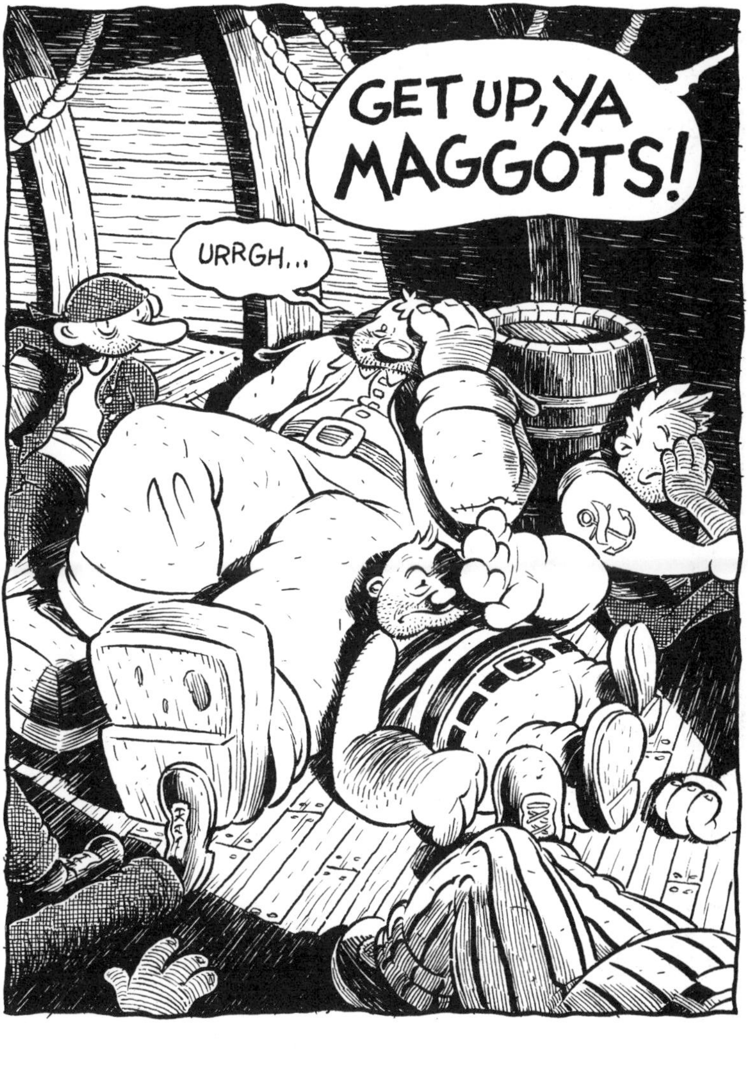
GET UP, YA MAGGOTS!
URRGH...

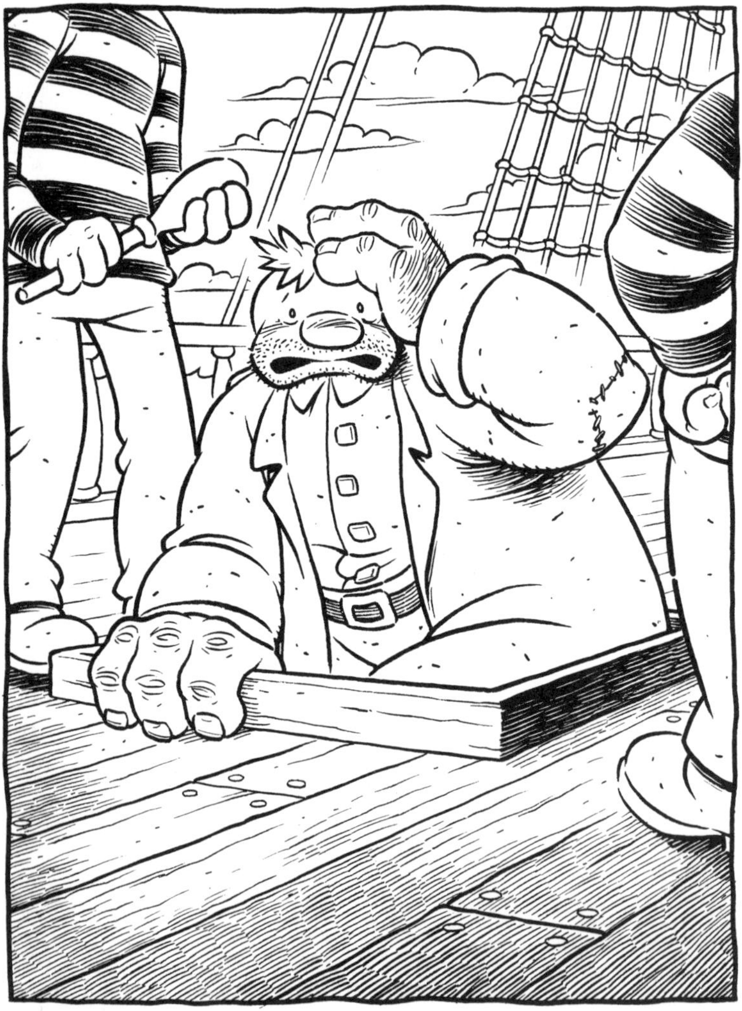

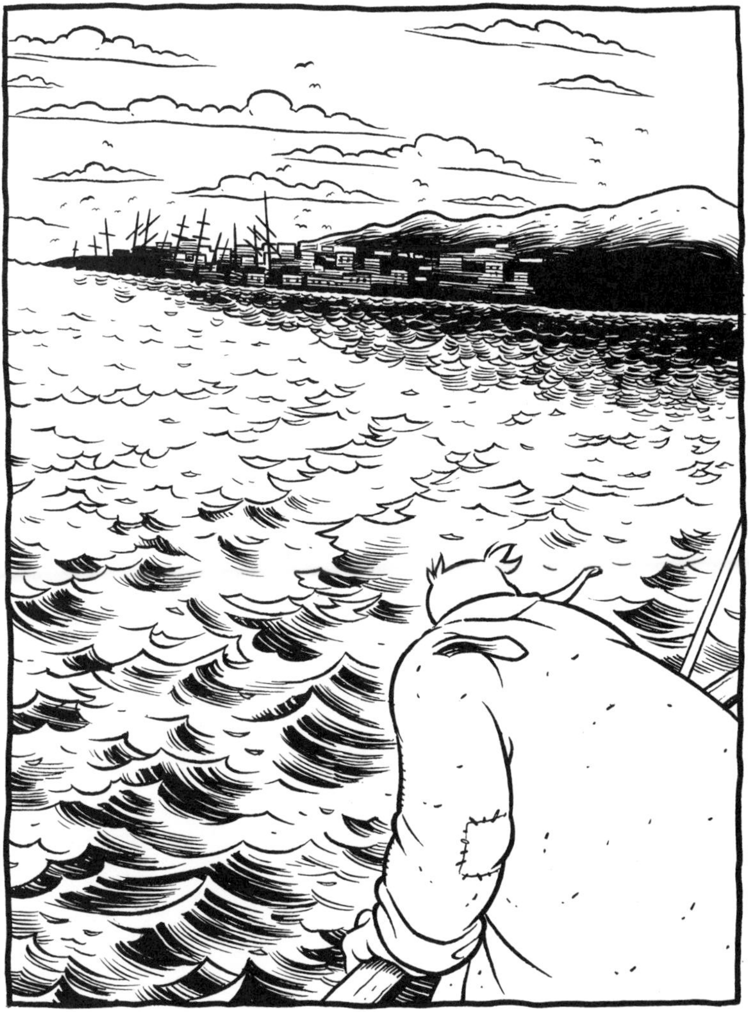

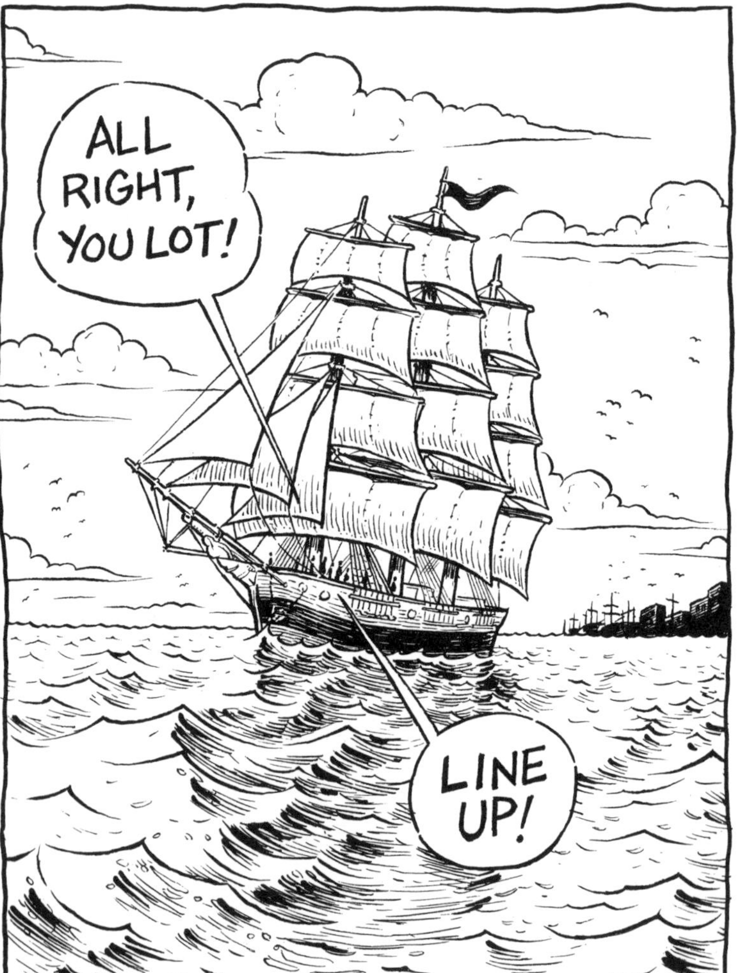
ALL RIGHT, YOU LOT!
LINE UP!

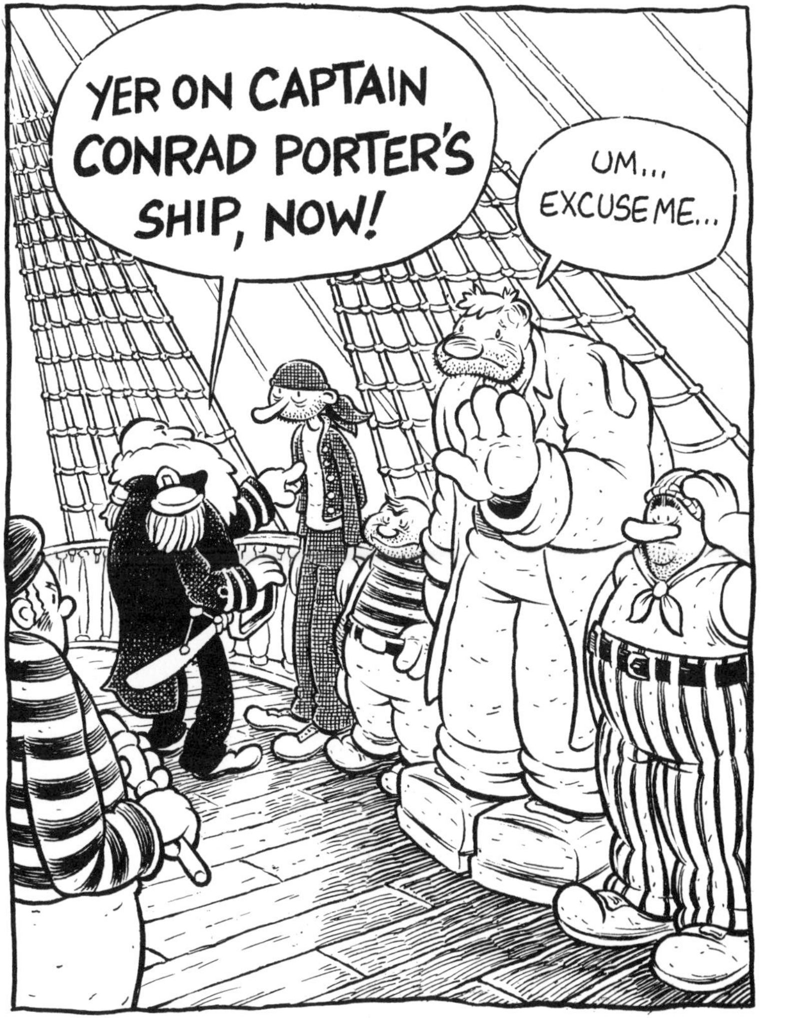
YER ON CAPTAIN CONRAD PORTER'S SHIP, NOW!
UM... EXCUSE ME...

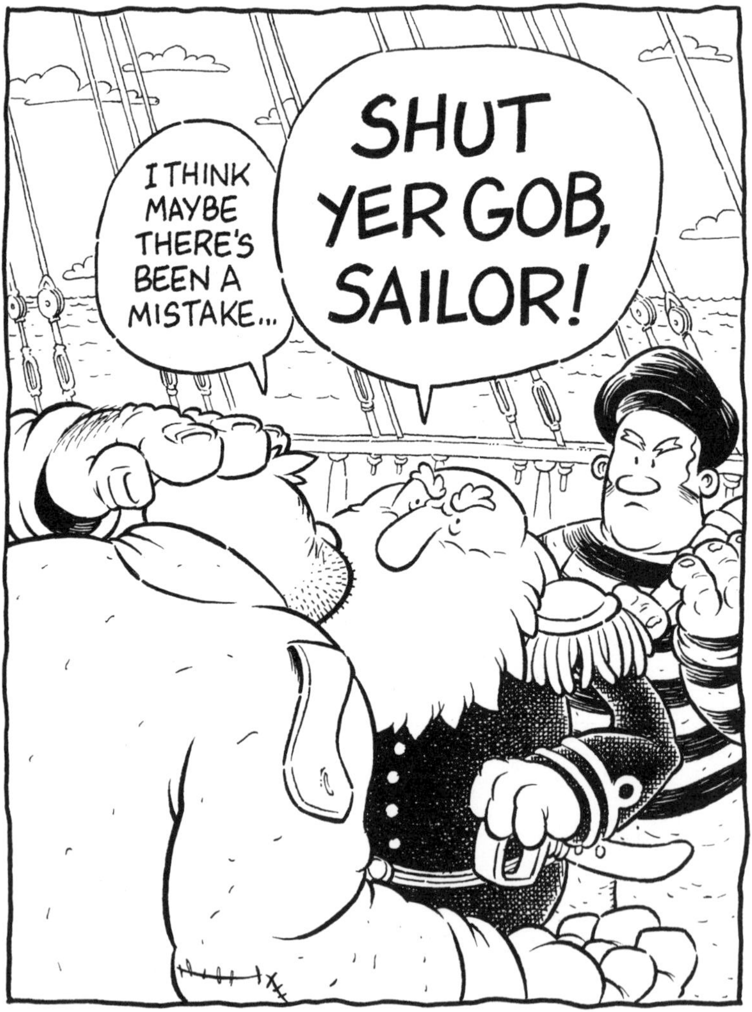
I THINK MAYBE THERE'S BEEN A MISTAKE...
SHUT YER GOB, SAILOR!

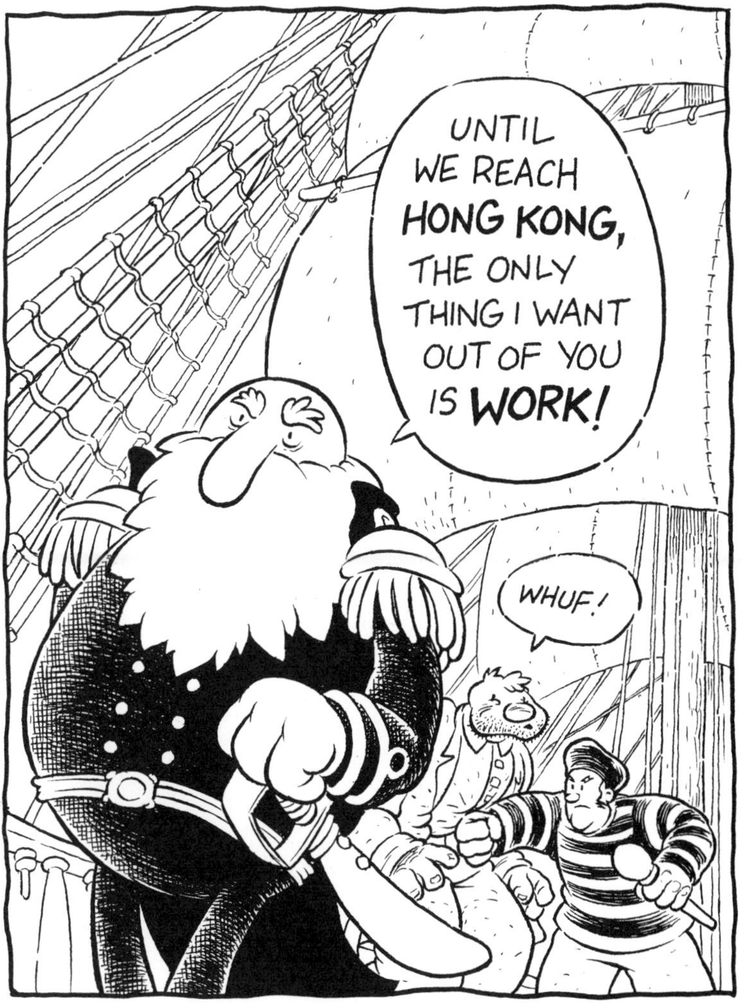
UNTIL WE REACH HONG KONG, THE ONLY THING I WANT OUT OF YOU IS WORK!
WHUF!

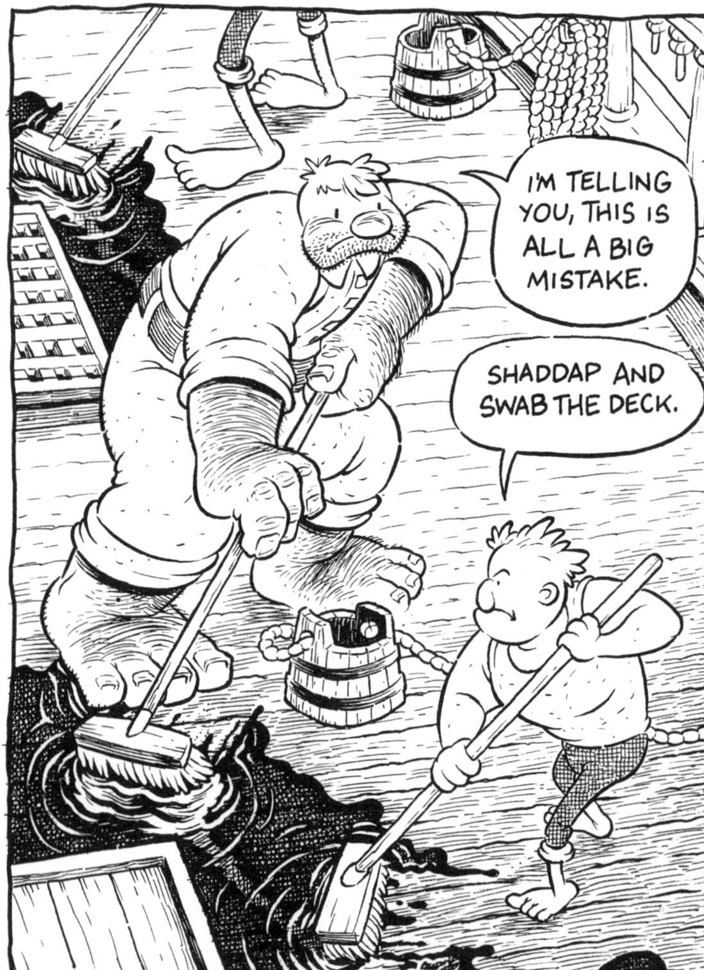
I'M TELLING YOU, THIS IS ALL A BIG MISTAKE.
SHADDAP AND SWAB THE DECK.

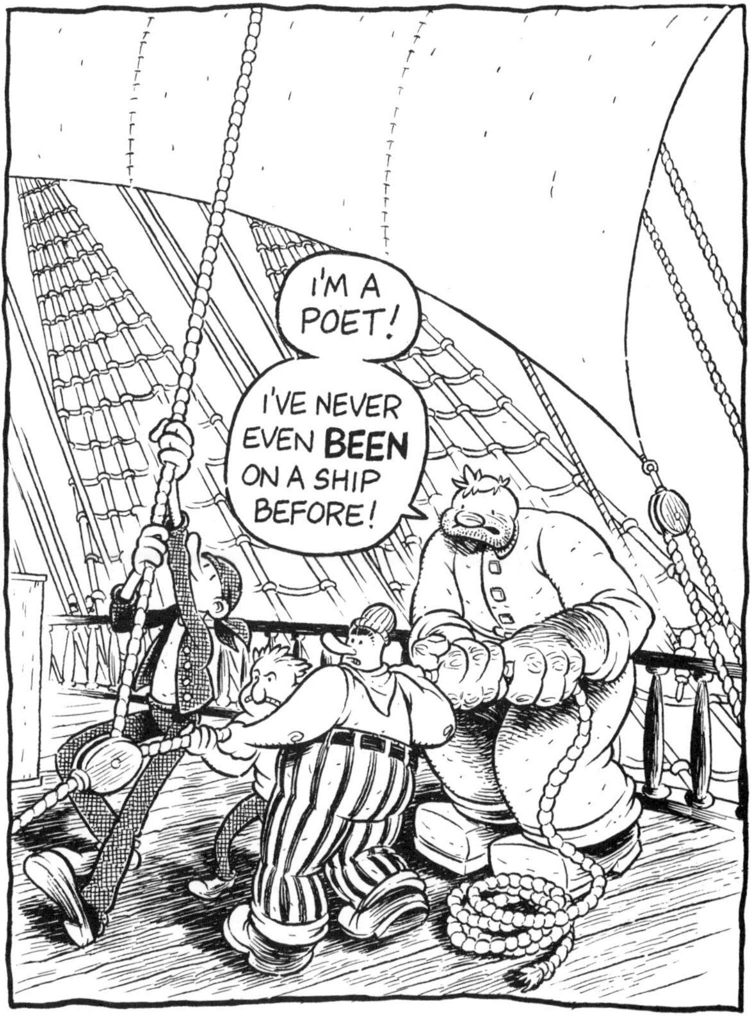
I'M A POET!
I'VE NEVER EVEN BEEN ON A SHIP BEFORE!

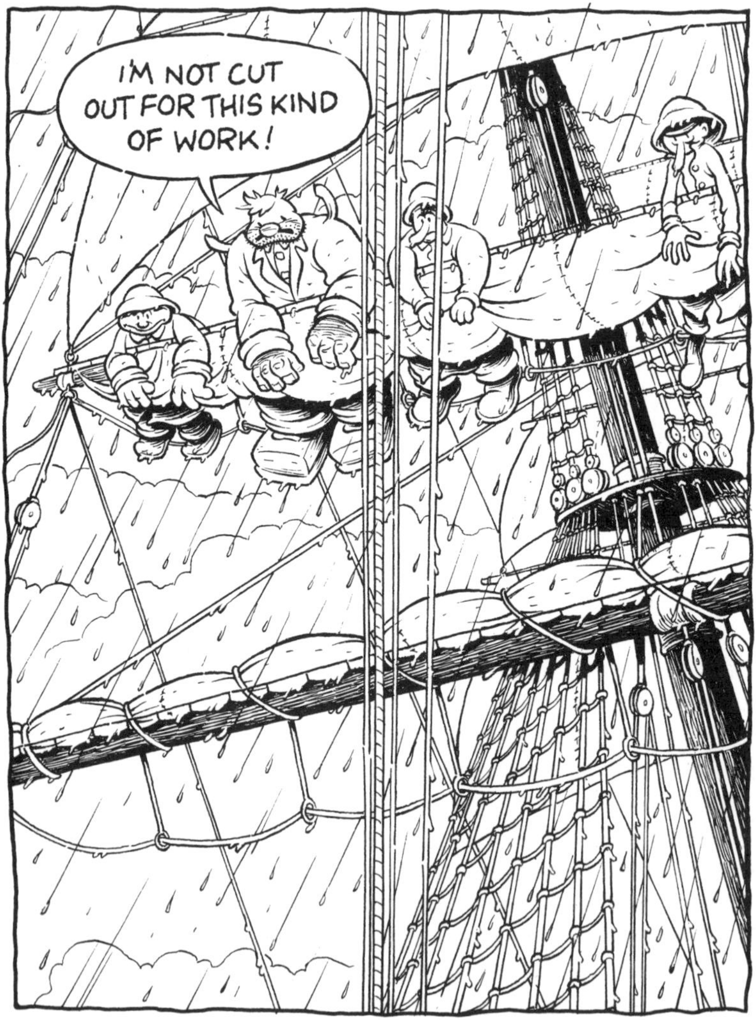
I'M NOT CUT OUT FOR THIS KIND OF WORK!

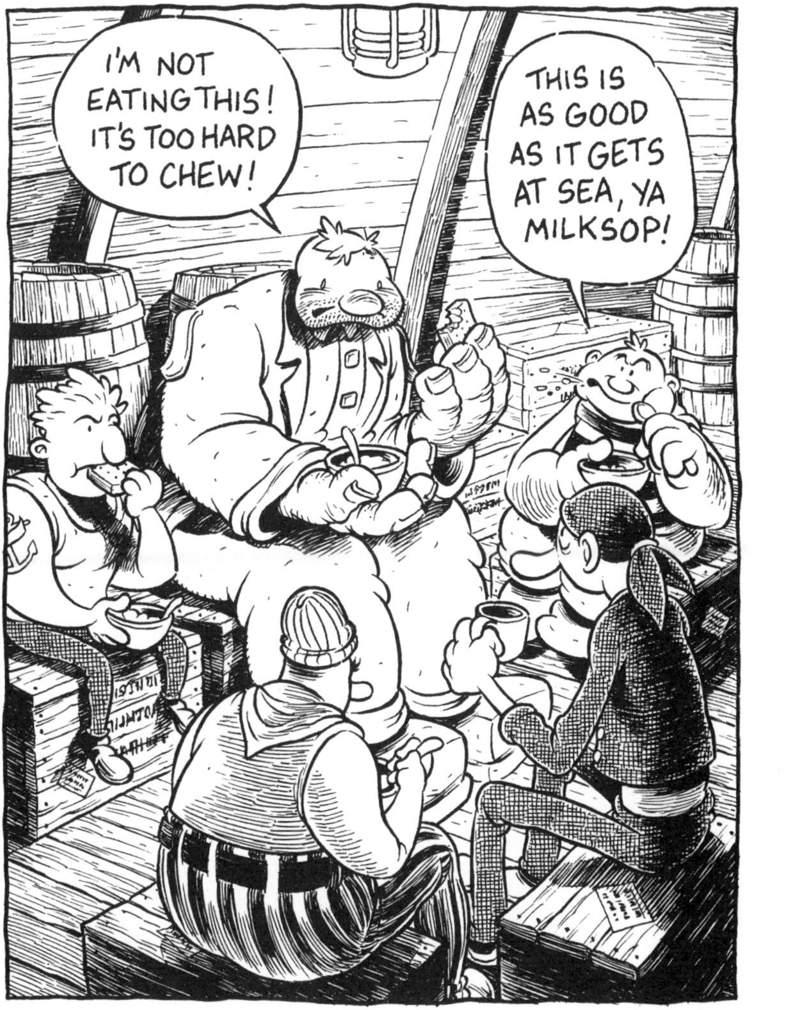
I'M NOT EATING THIS! IT'S TOO HARD TO CHEW!
THIS IS AS GOOD AS IT GETS AT SEA, YA MILKSOP!

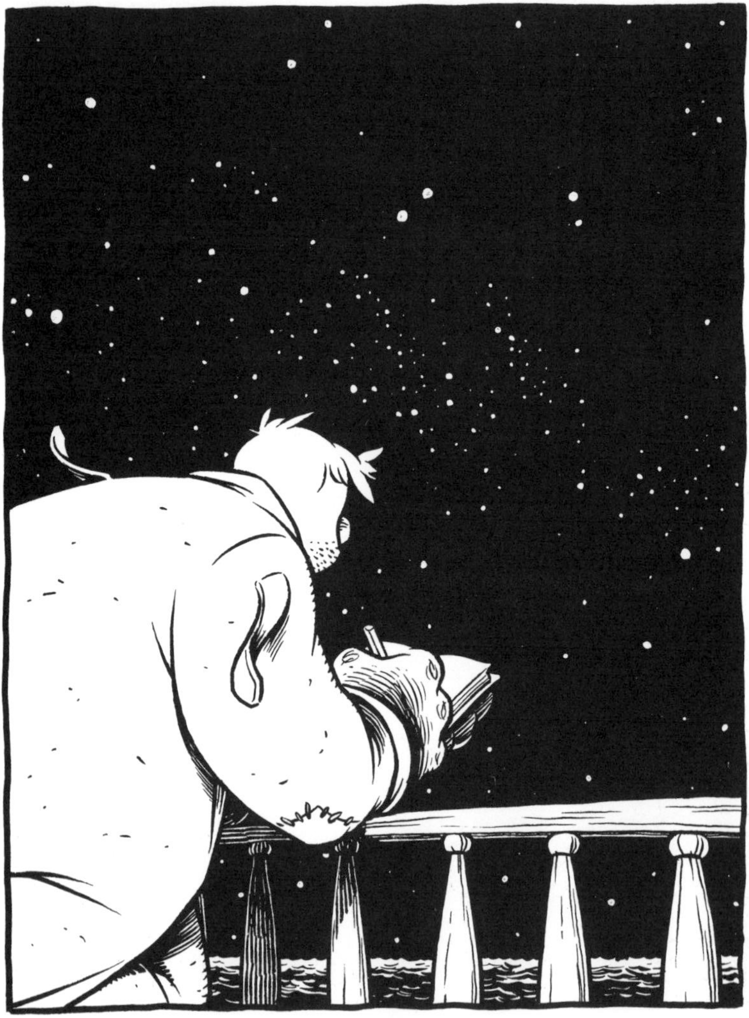

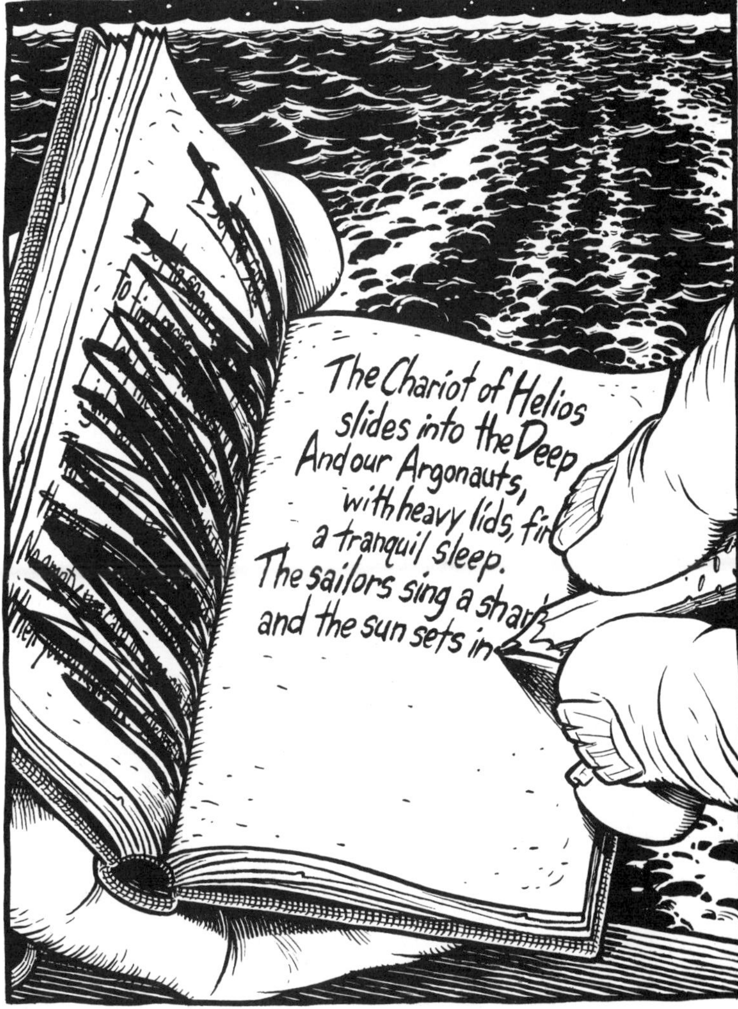
The Chariot of Helios
slides into the Deep
And our Argonauts,
with heavy lids, fir
a tranquil sleep.
The sailors sing a shar
and the sun sets in

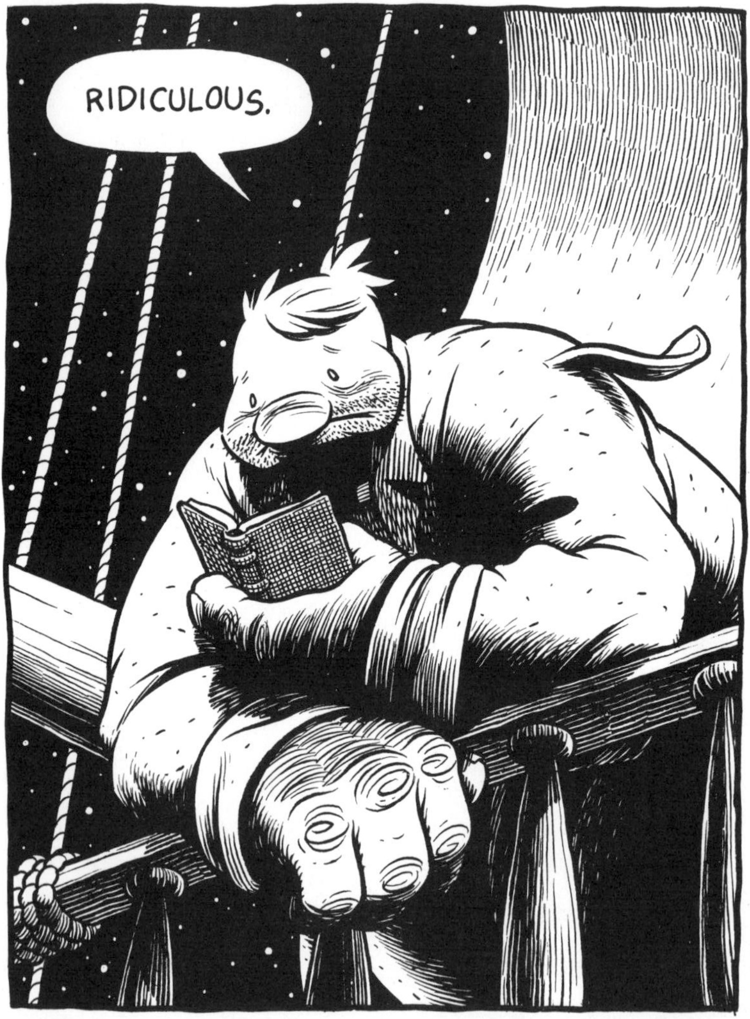
RIDICULOUS.

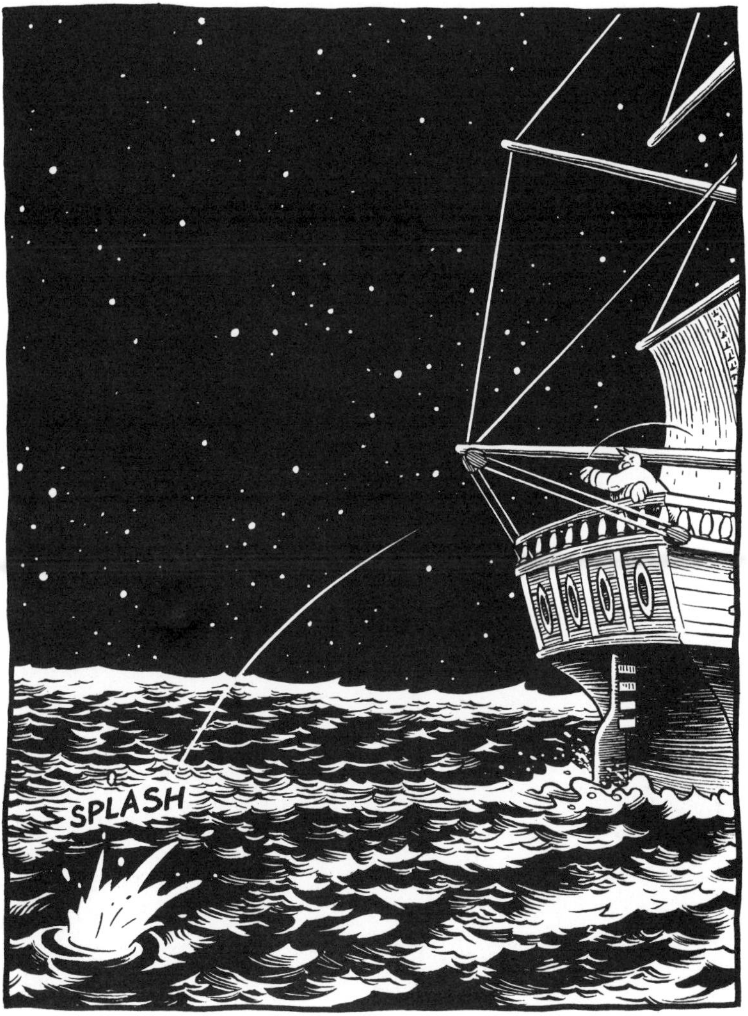
SPLASH

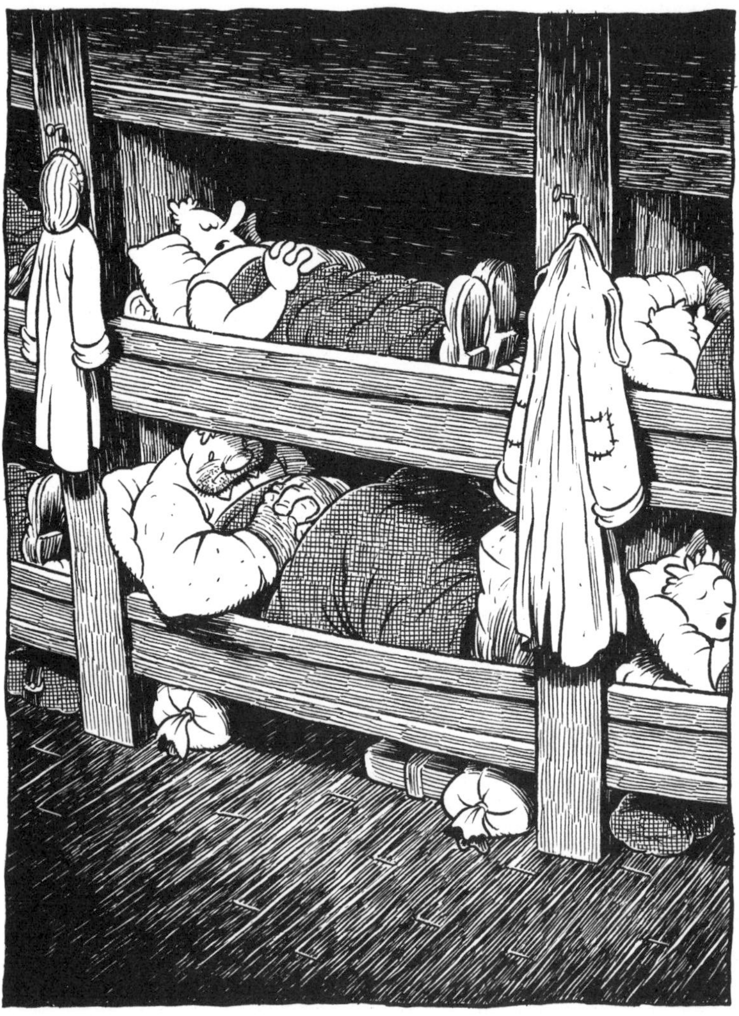

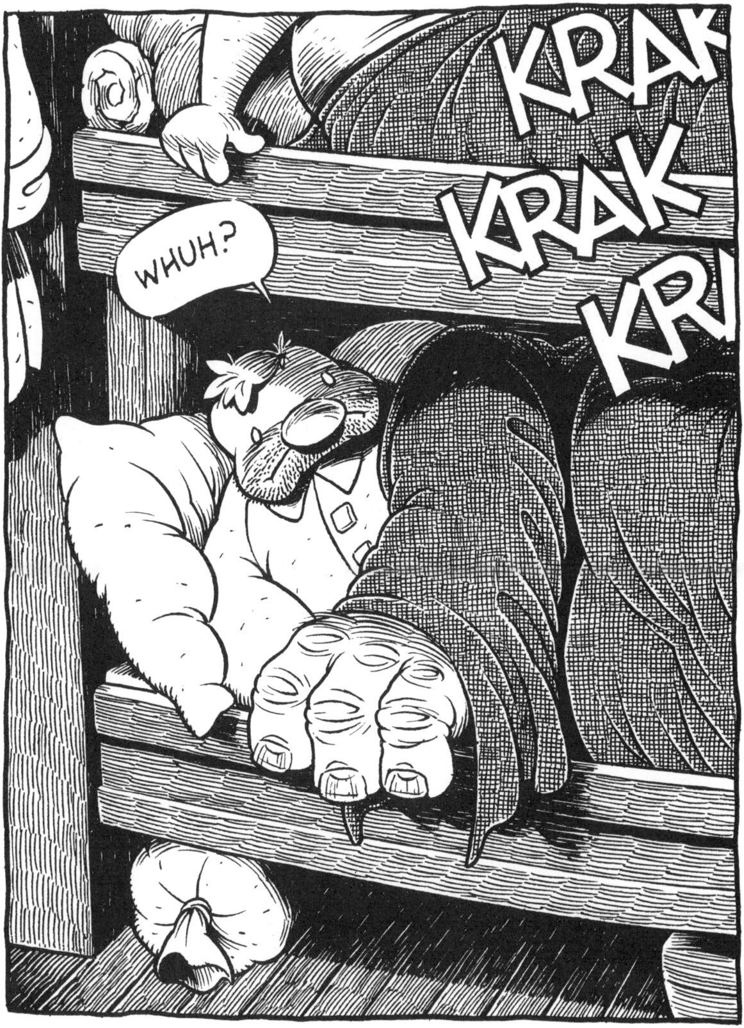
KRAK
KRAK
KR
WHUH?

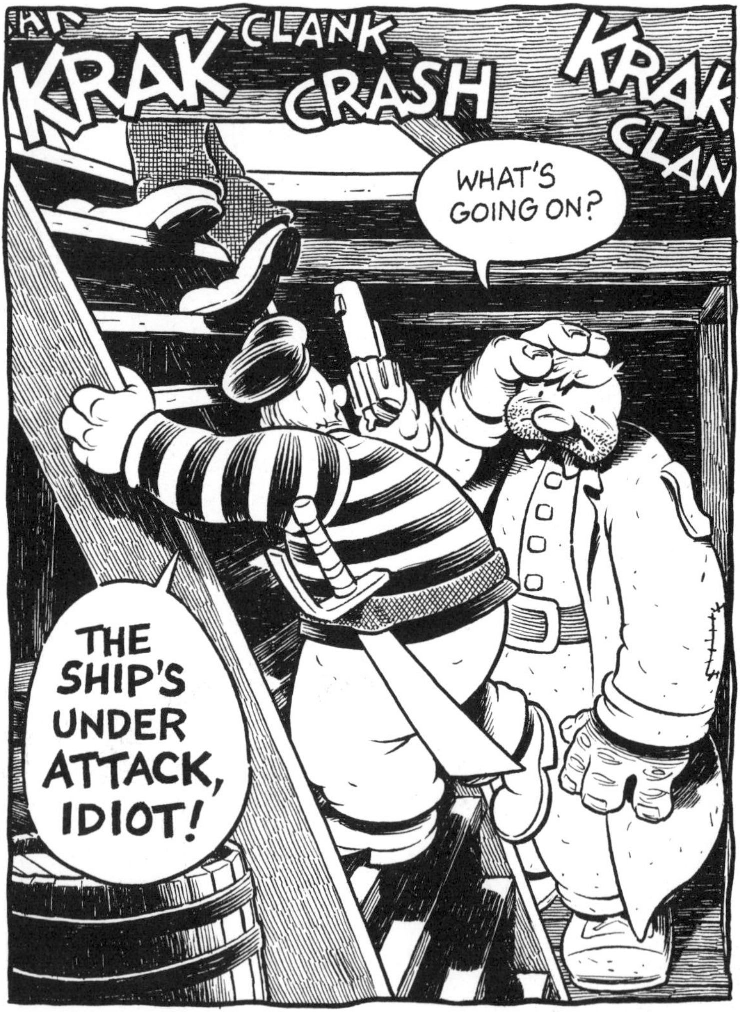
KRAK
CLANK
CRASH
KRAK
CLAN
WHAT'S GOING ON?
THE SHIP'S UNDER ATTACK, IDIOT!

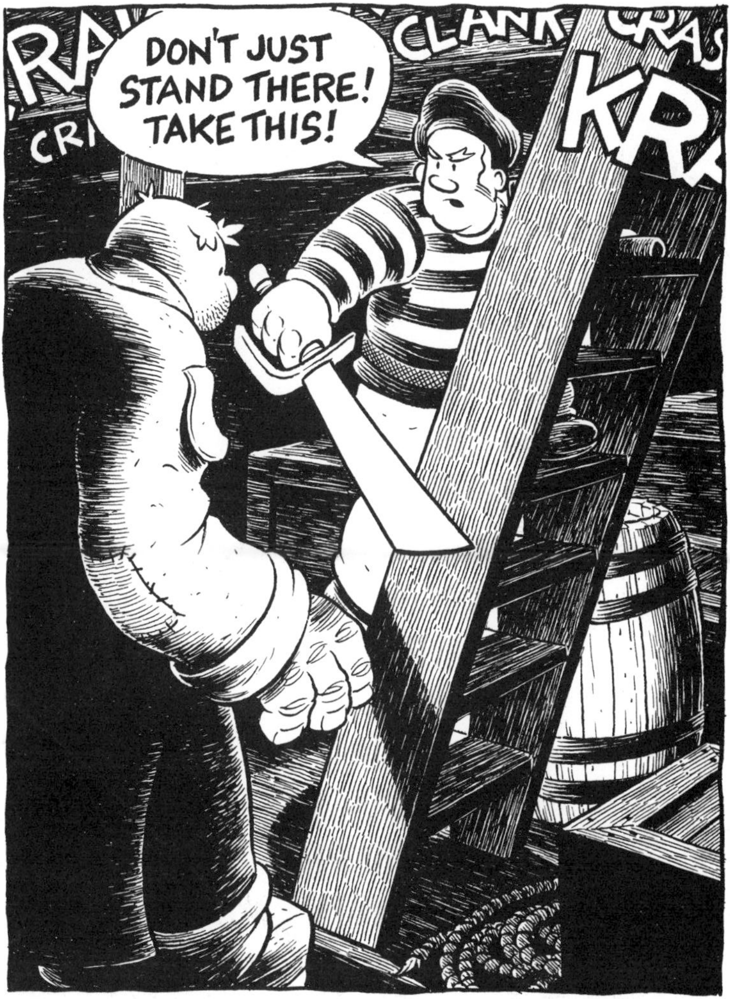
DON'T JUST STAND THERE! TAKE THIS!
CLANK

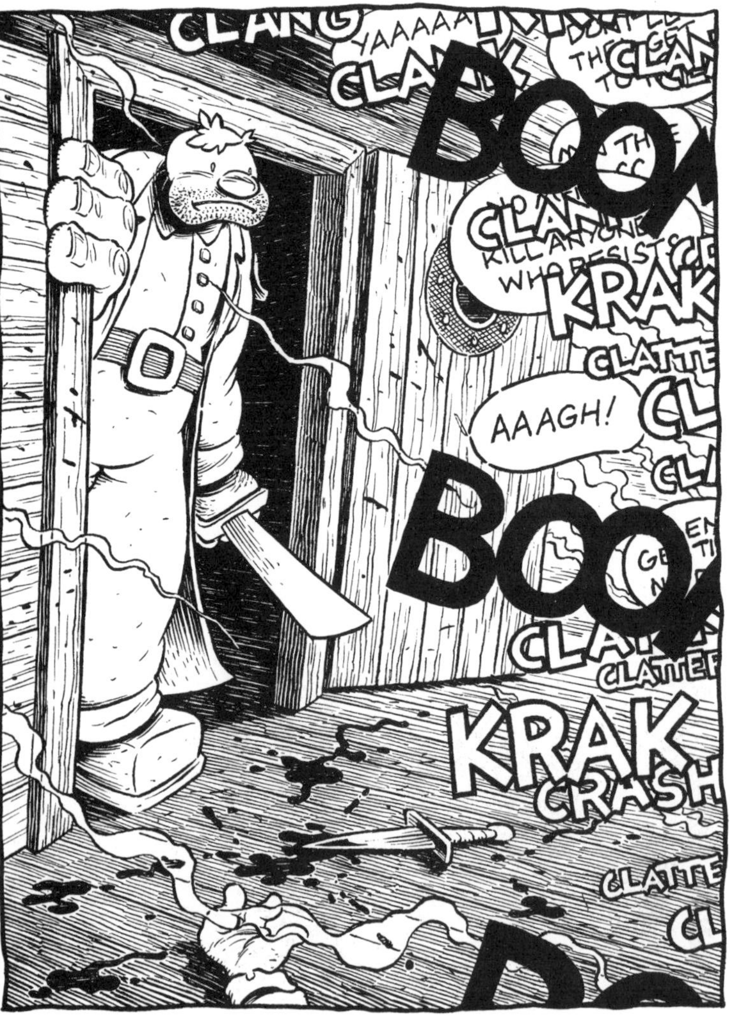
CLANG
YAAAAA
AAAGH!
KRAK
CRASH

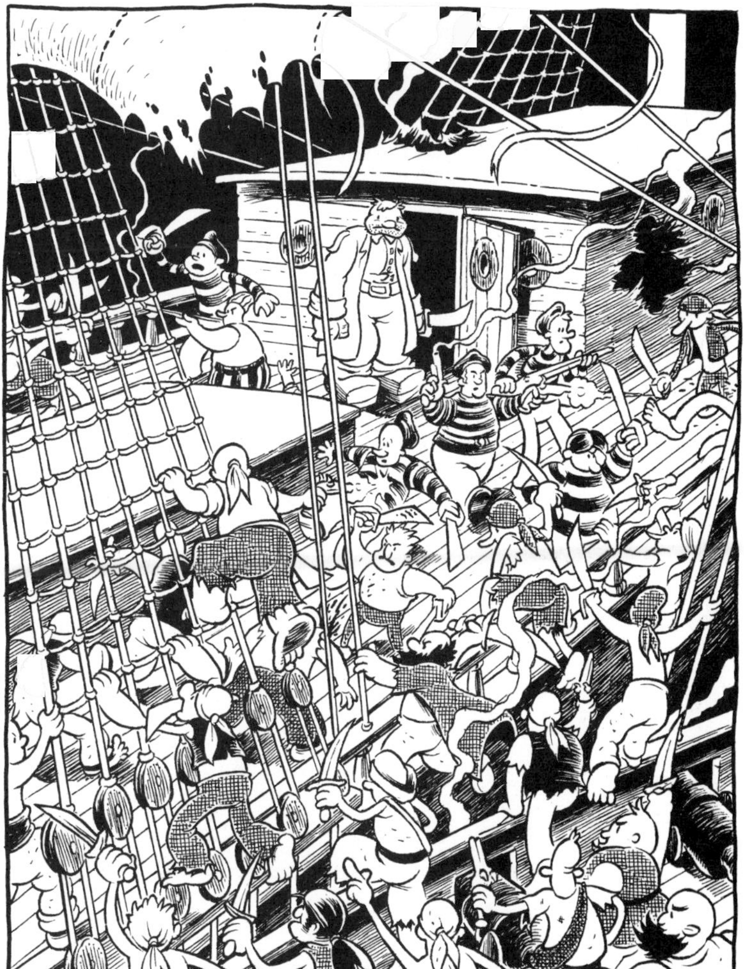

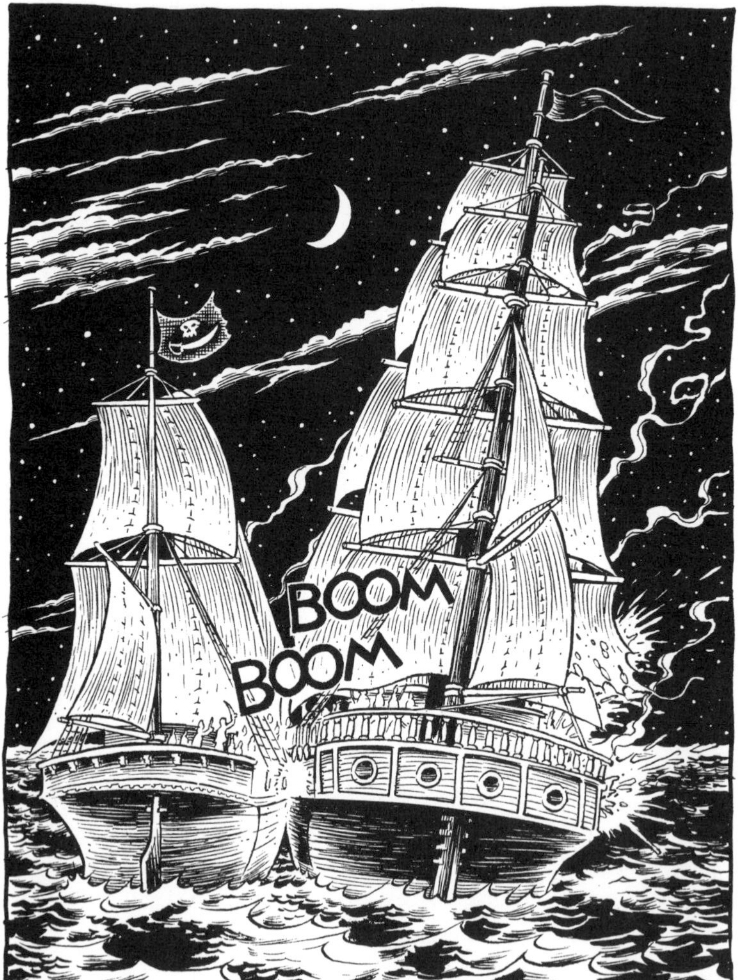
BOOM
BOOM

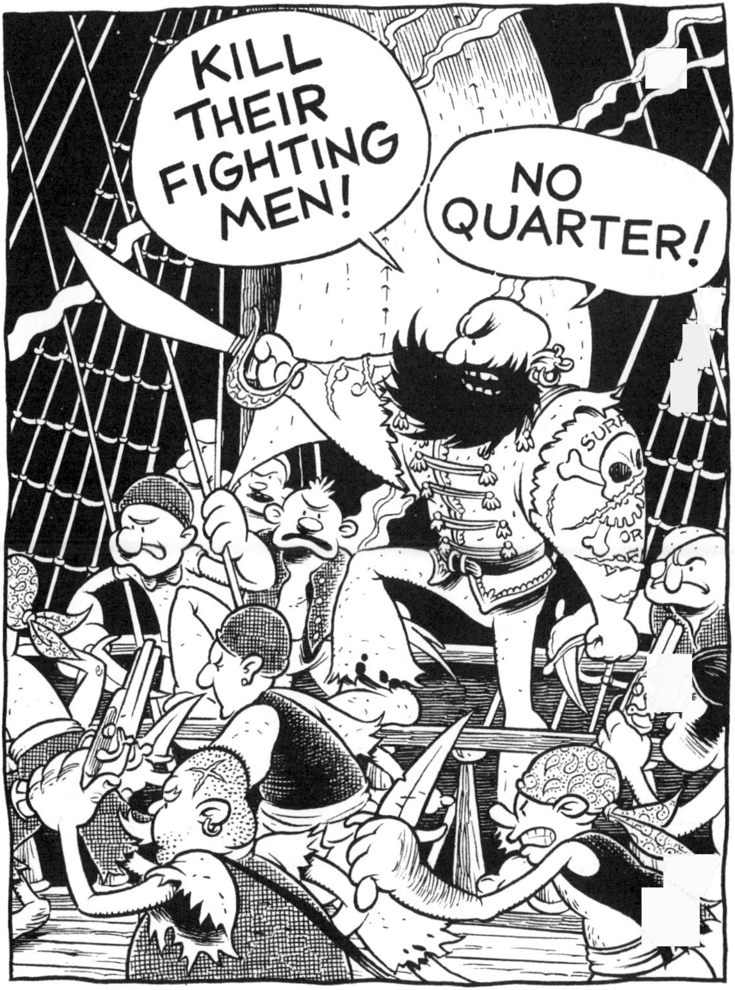
KILL THEIR FIGHTING MEN!
NO QUARTER!

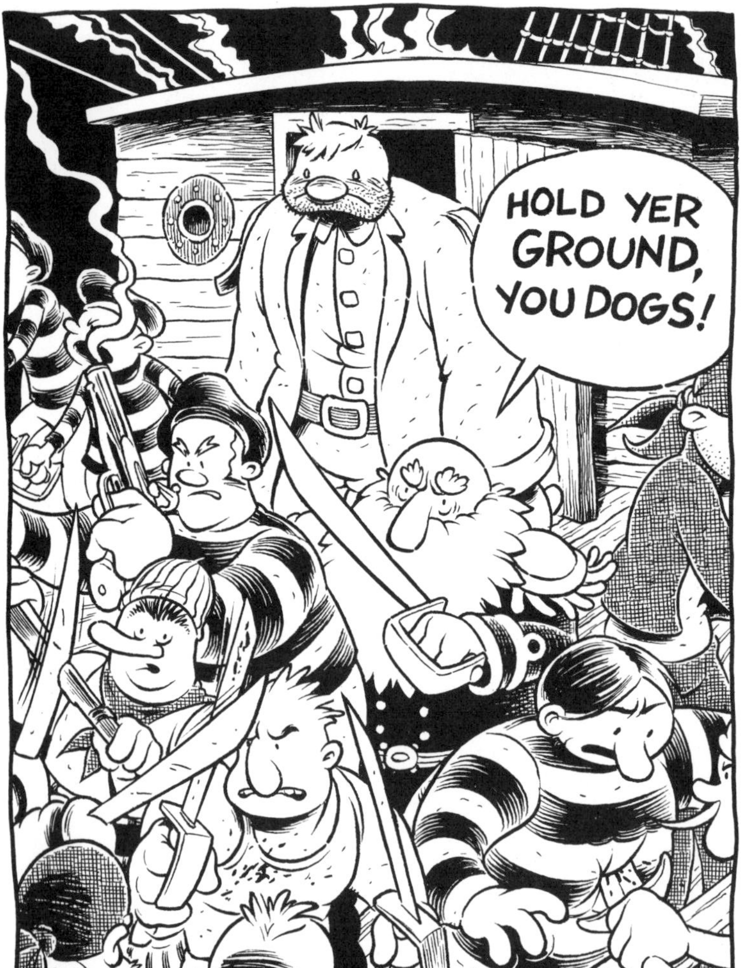
HOLD YER GROUND, YOU DOGS!

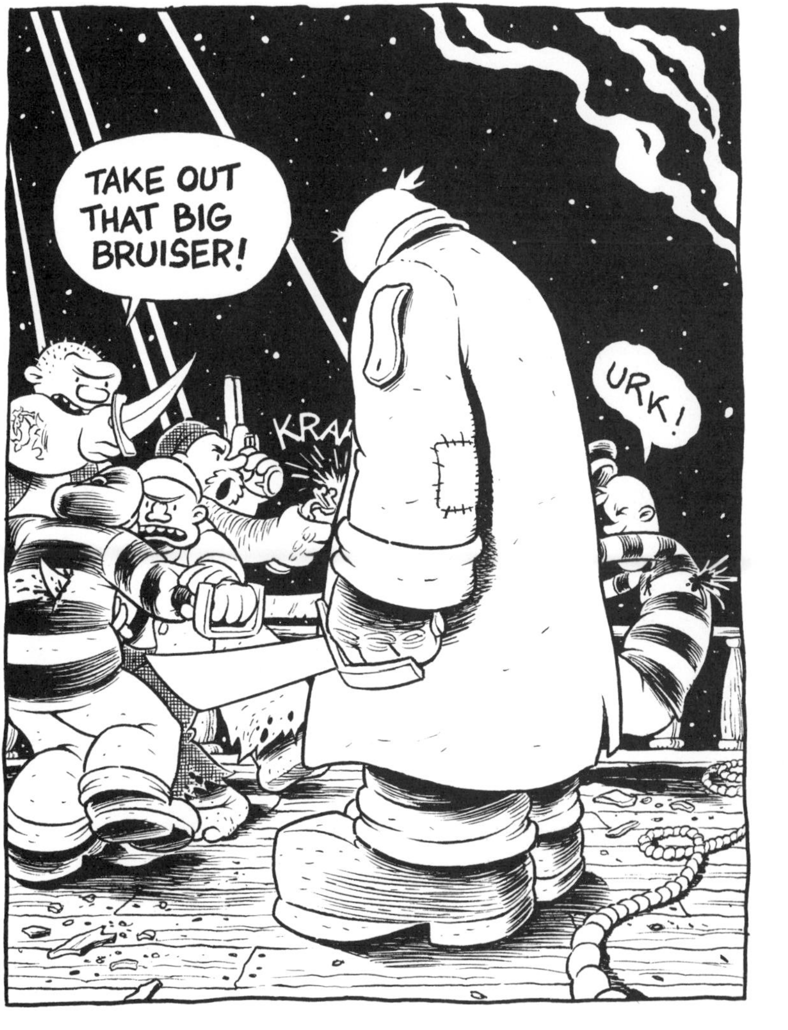
TAKE OUT THAT BIG BRUISER!
KRAK
URK!

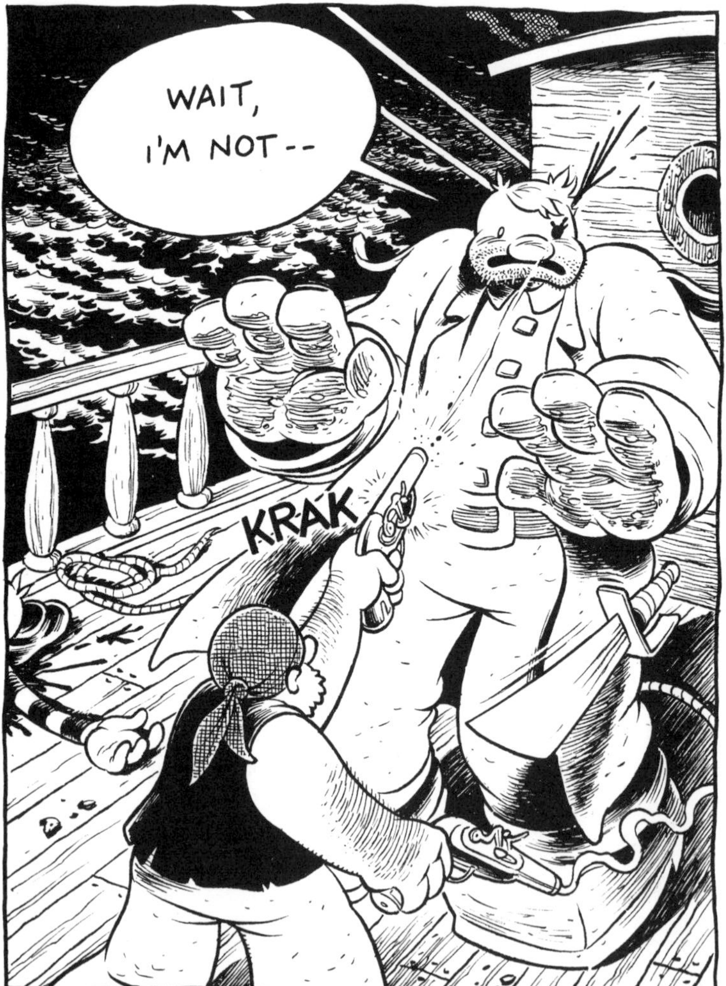
WAIT, I'M NOT --
KRAK

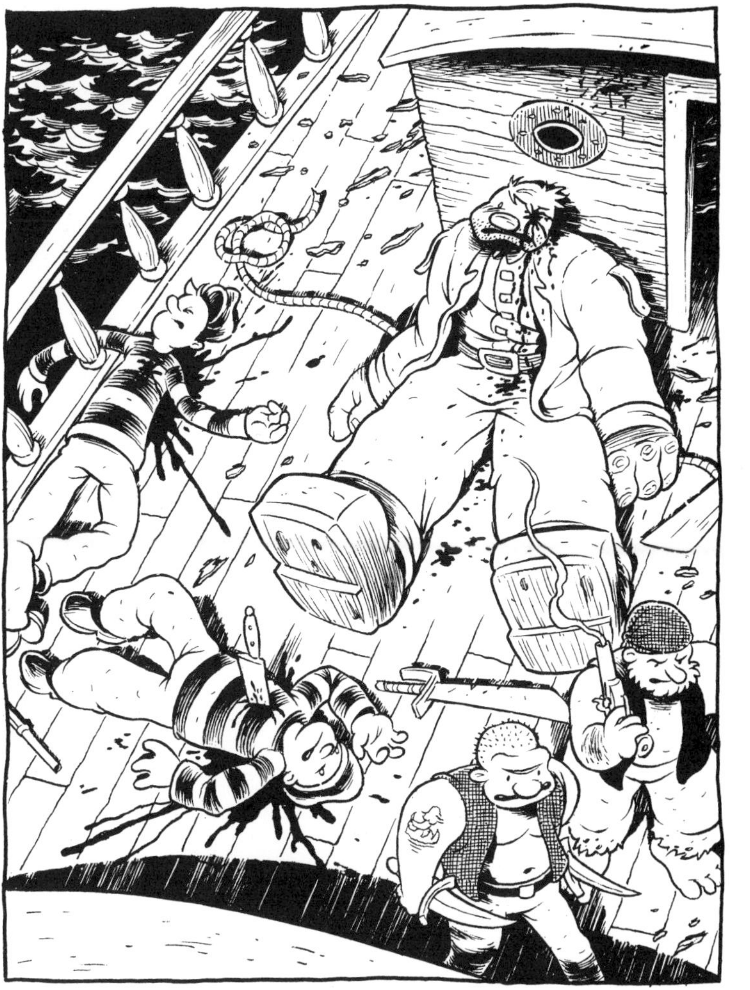

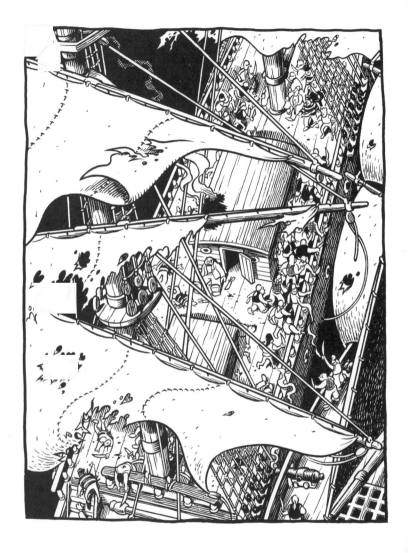

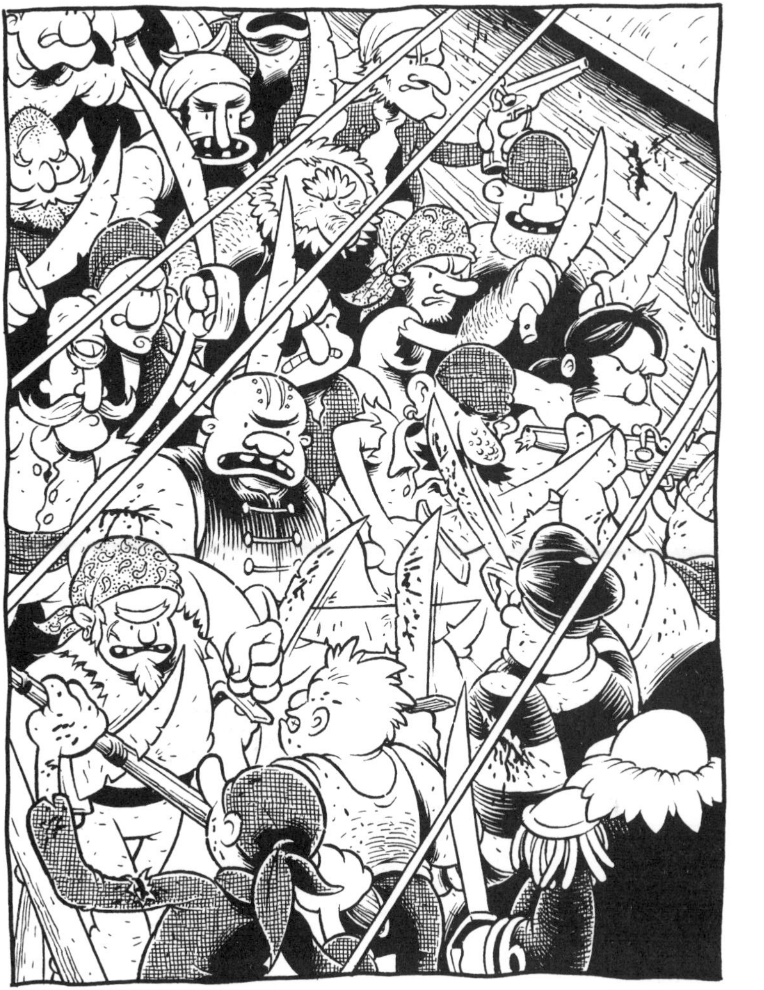

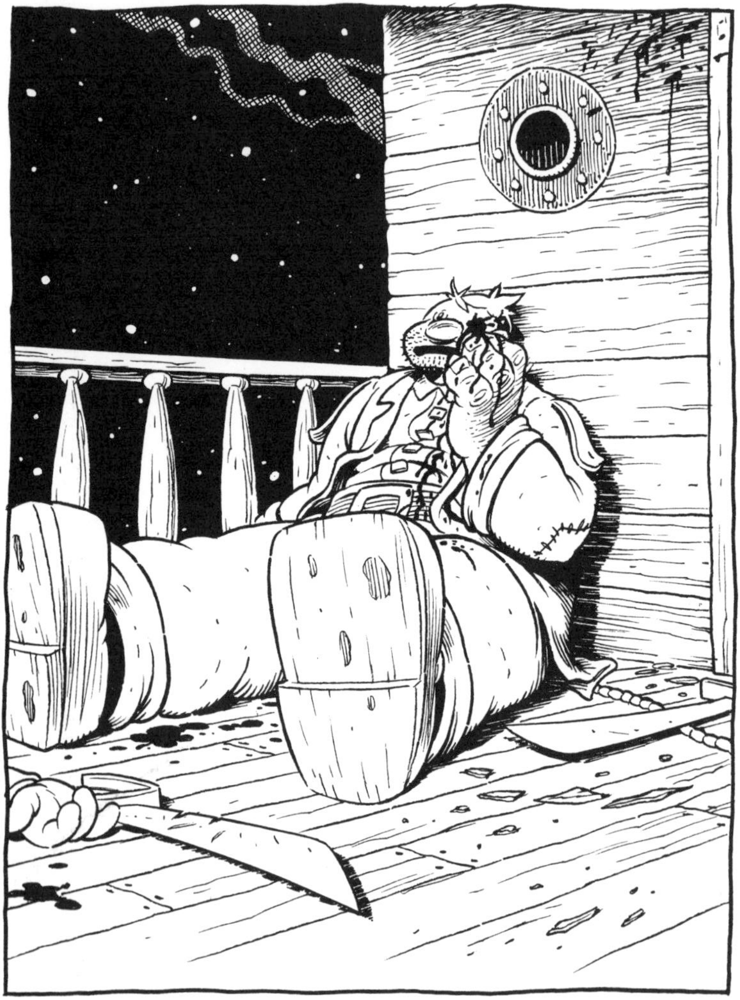

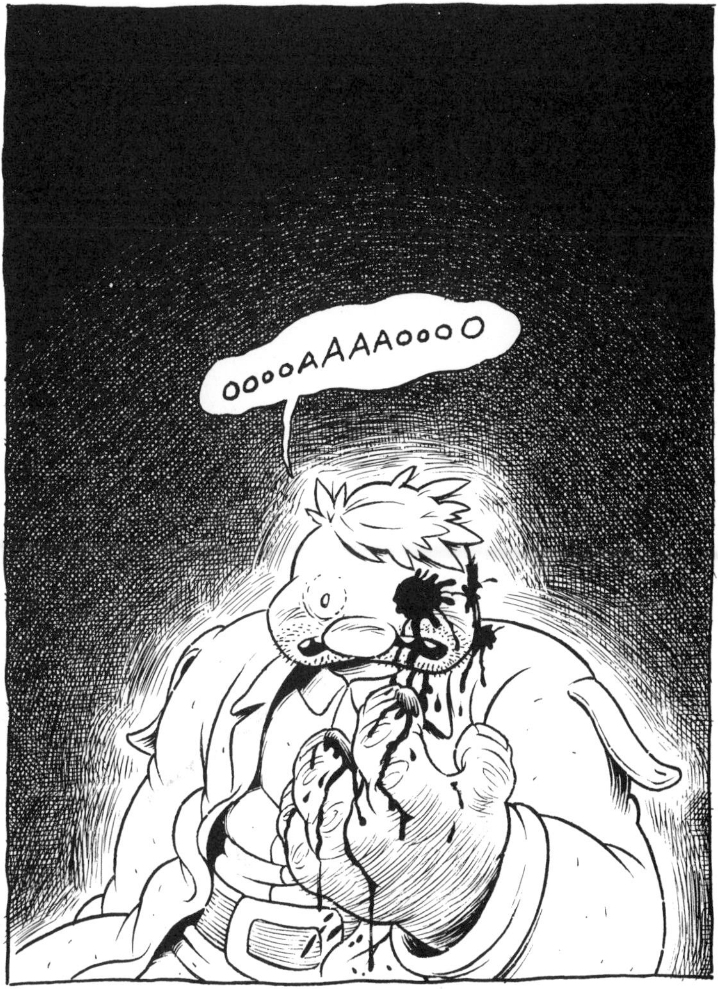
OOOOAAAAOOOO

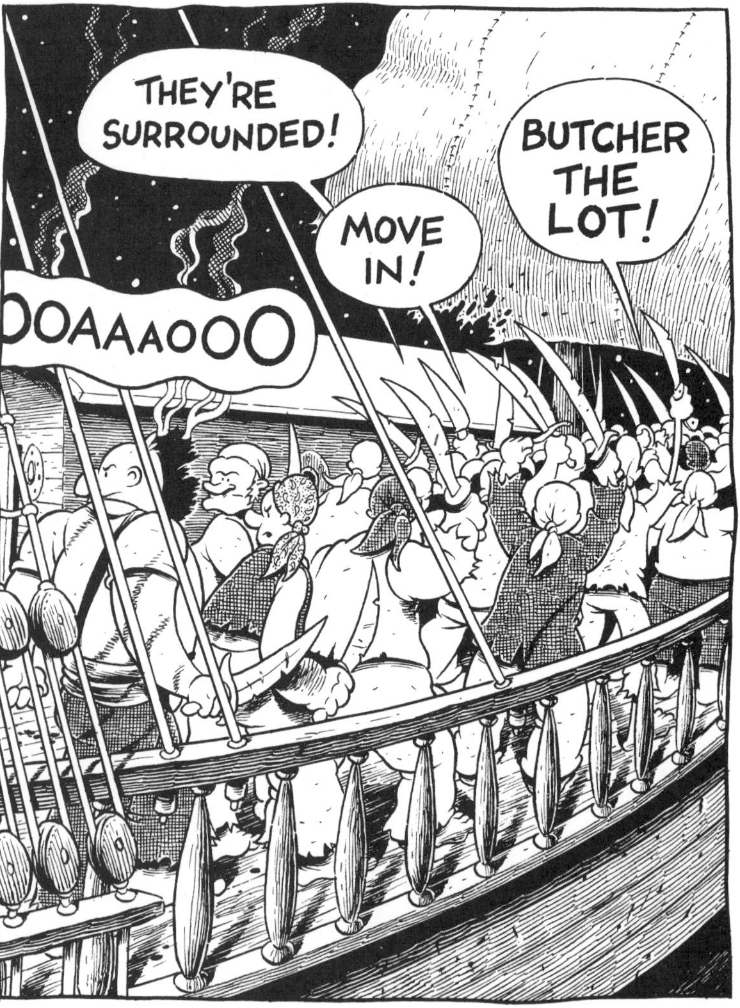
OOAAAAOOO
THEY'RE SURROUNDED!
MOVE IN!
BUTCHER THE LOT!

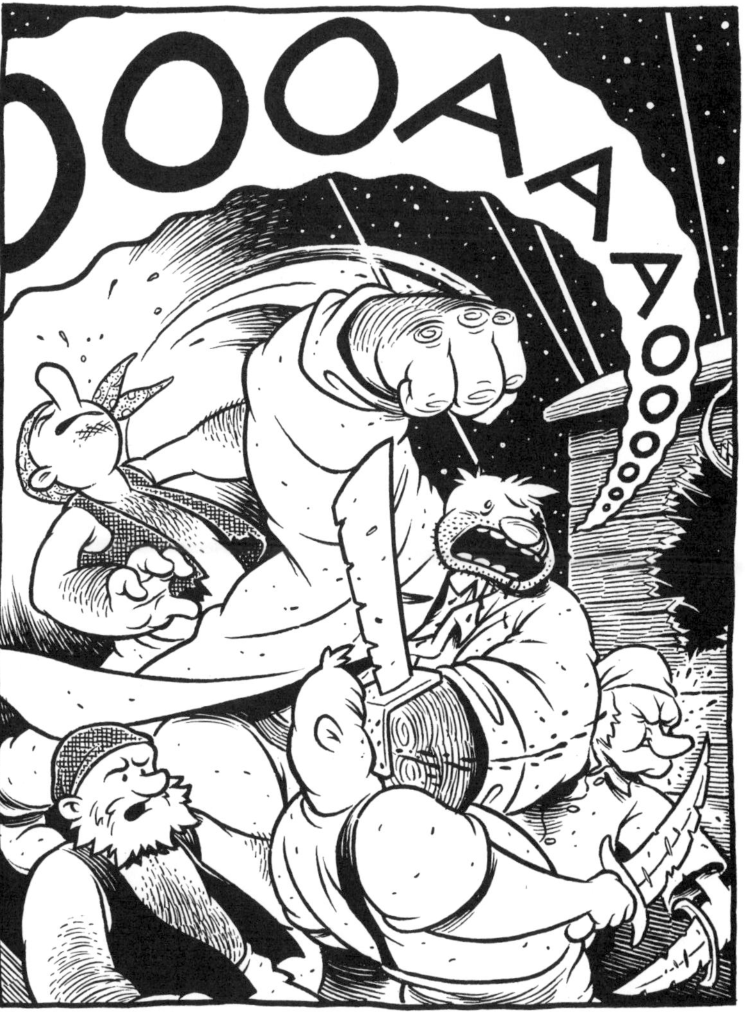
OOOAAAAOOOOOO

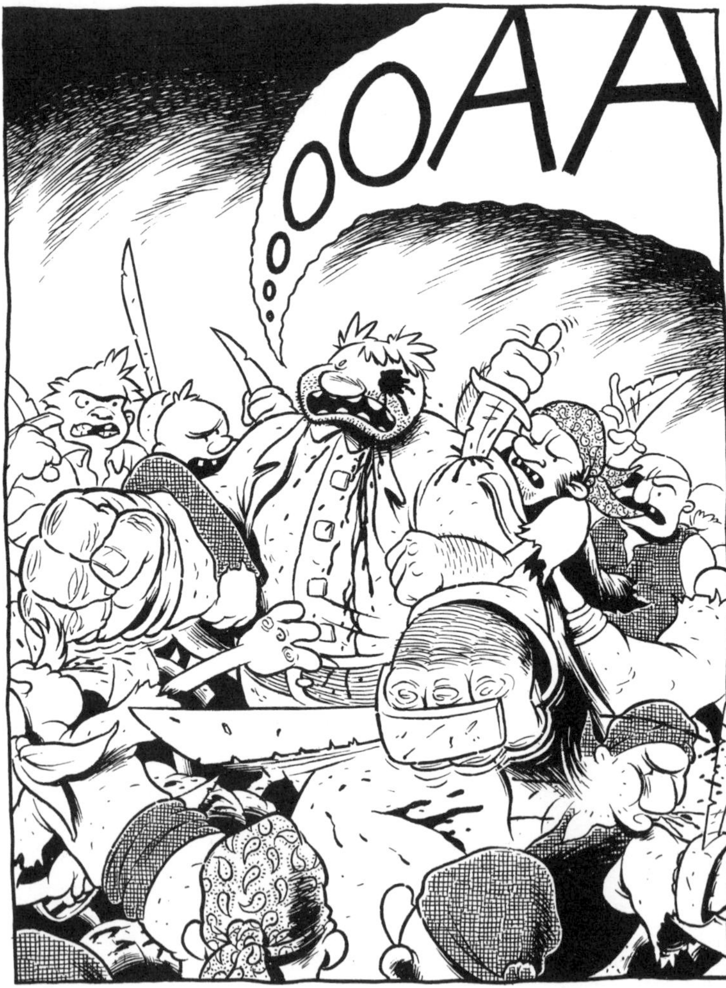
OOOOOOOAA

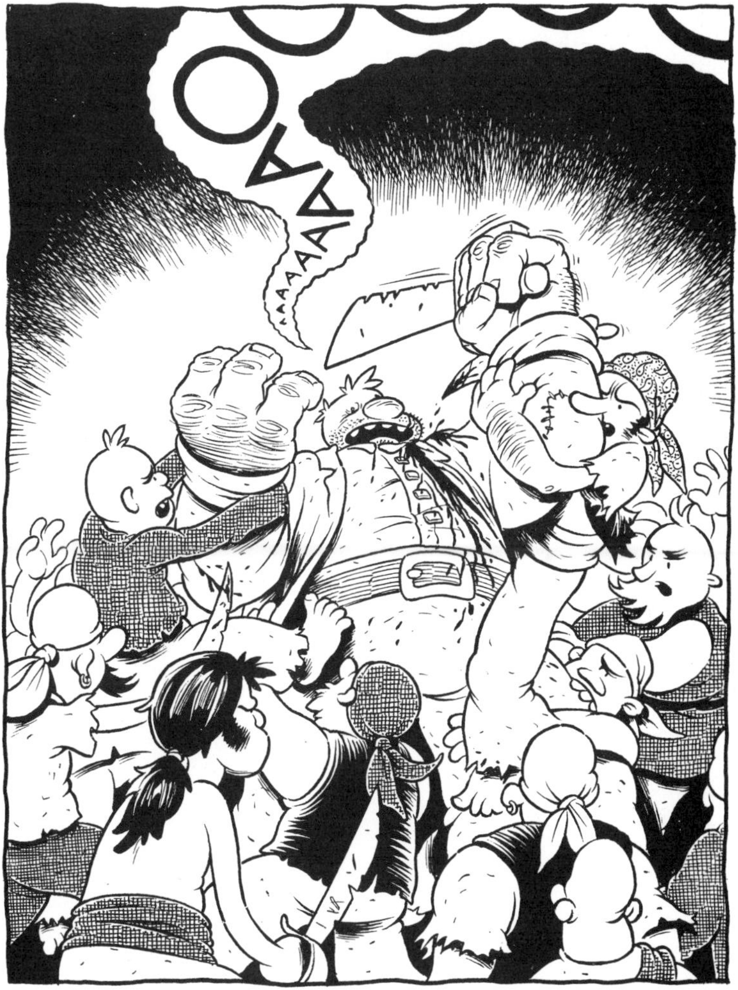
AAAAAAAAAAAAOOOOO

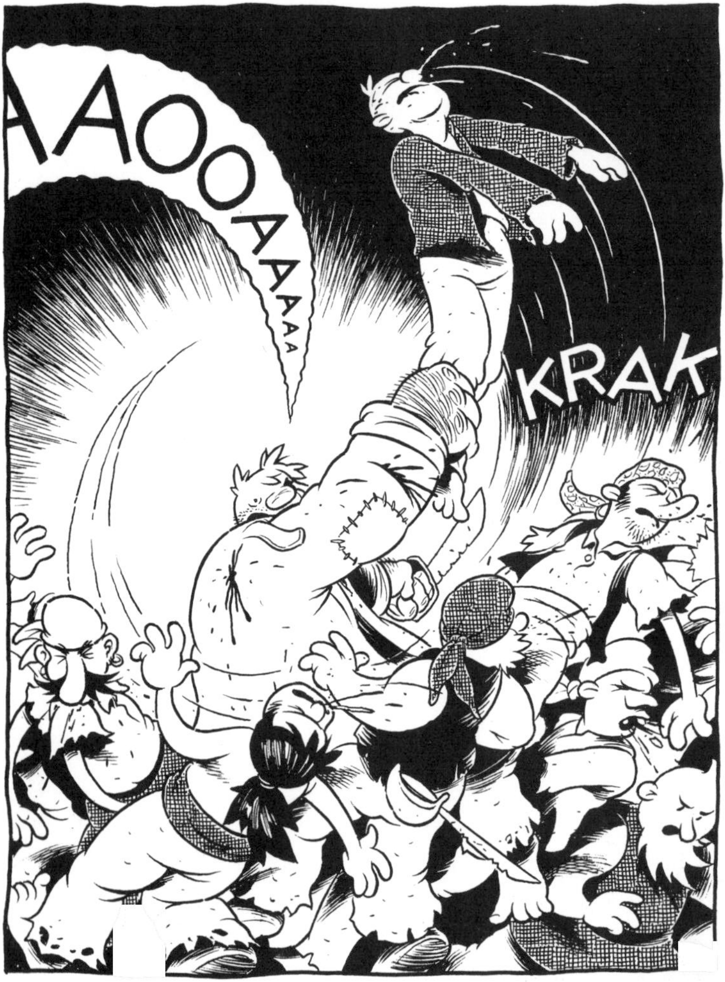
AAOOAAAAA
KRAK

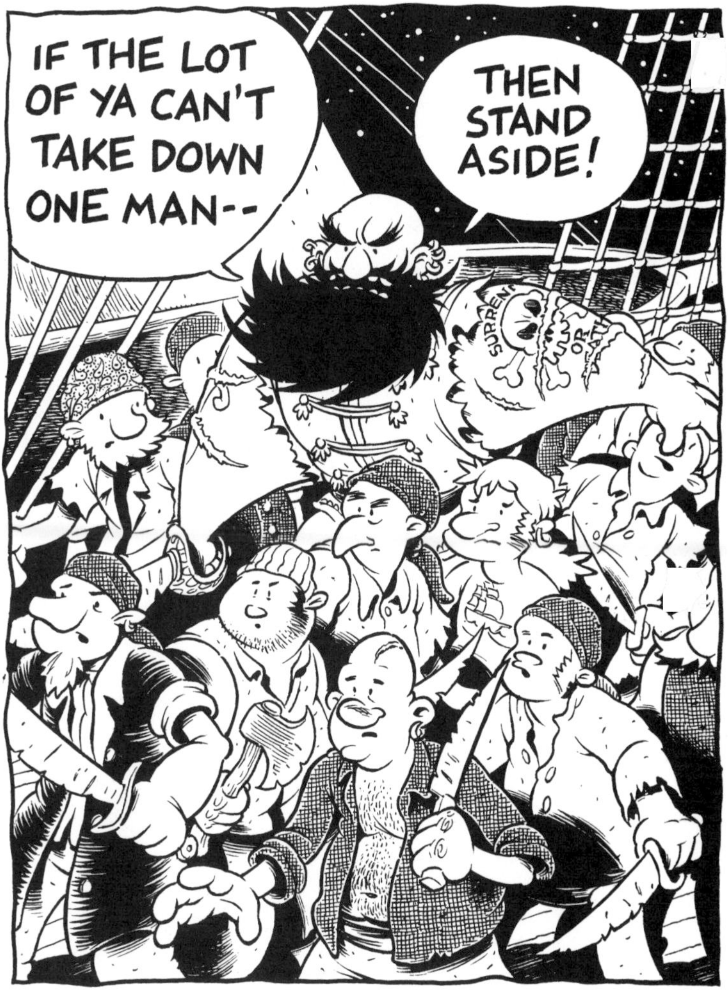
IF THE LOT OF YA CAN'T TAKE DOWN ONE MAN--
THEN STAND ASIDE!

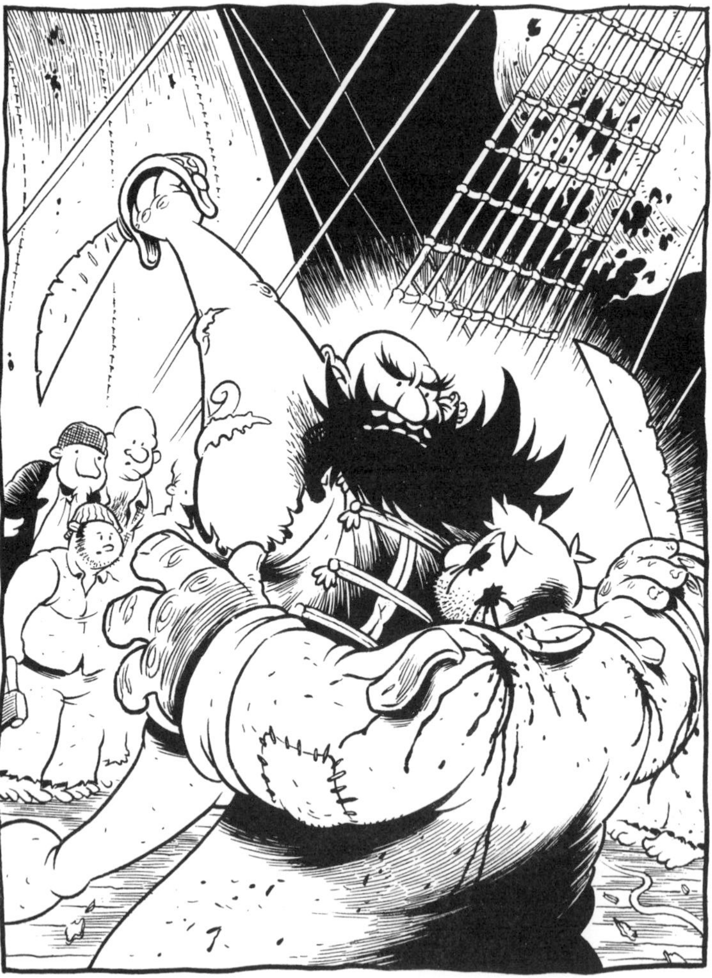

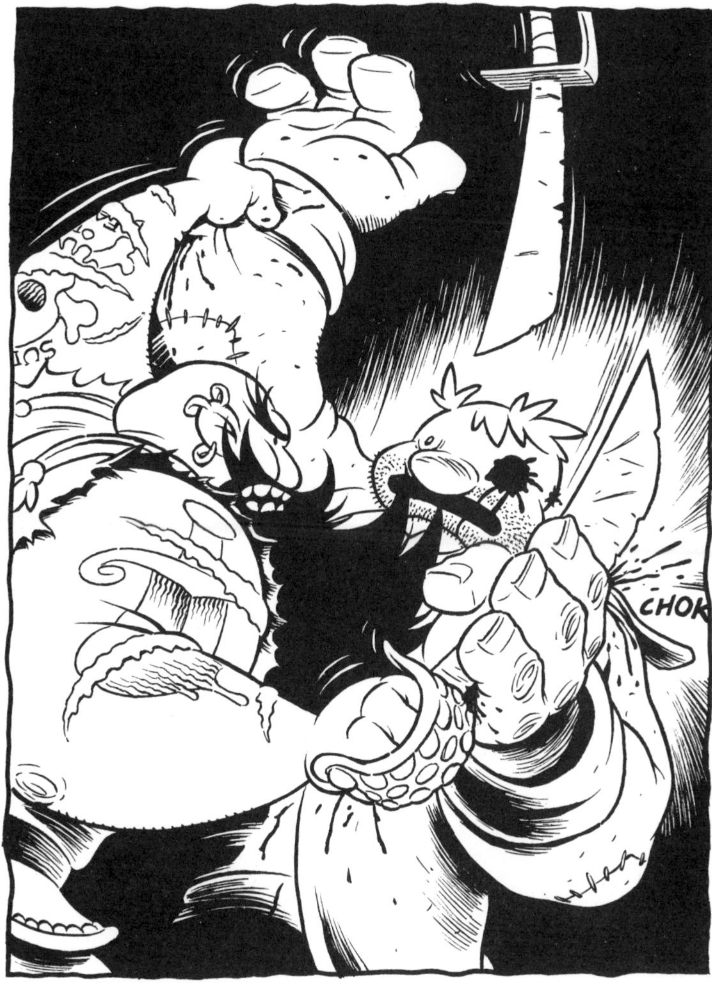
CHOK

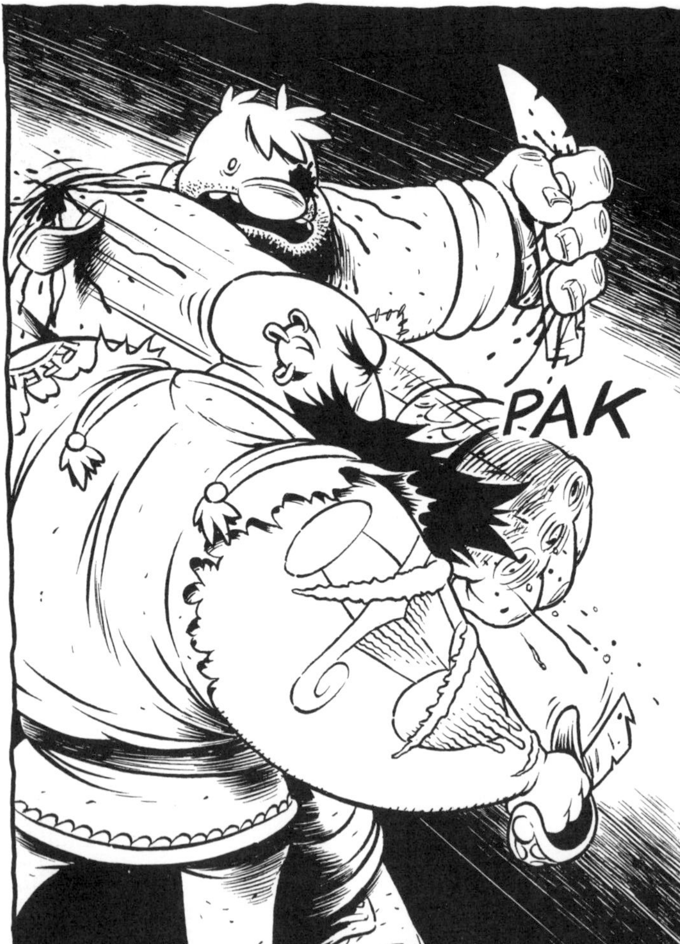
PAK

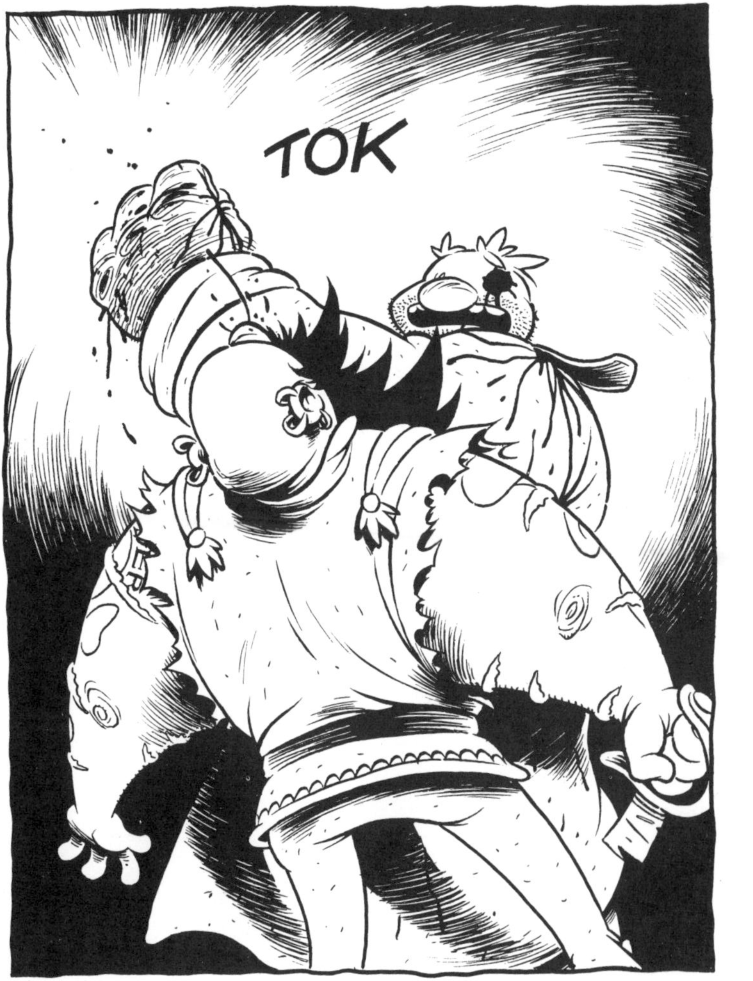
TOK

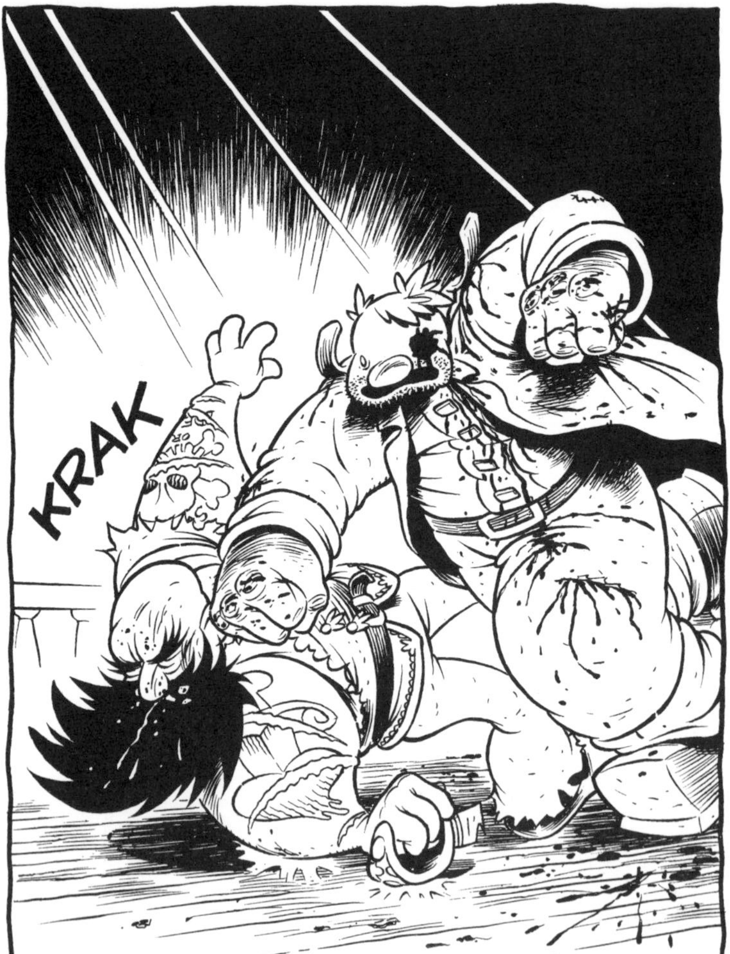
KRAK

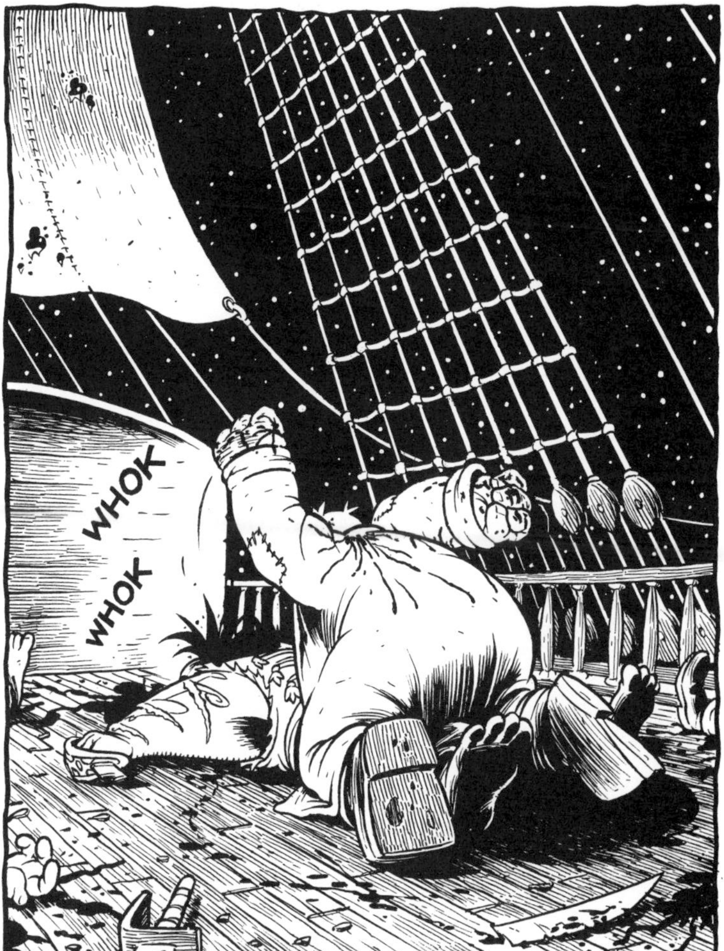
WHOK
WHOK

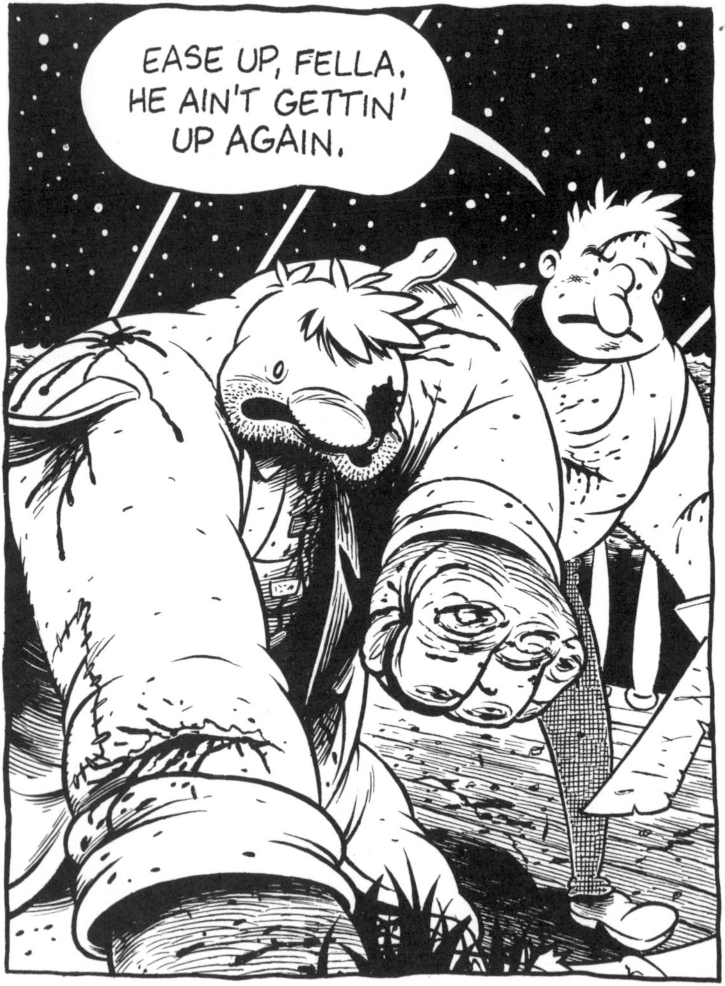
EASE UP, FELLA. HE AIN'T GETTIN' UP AGAIN.

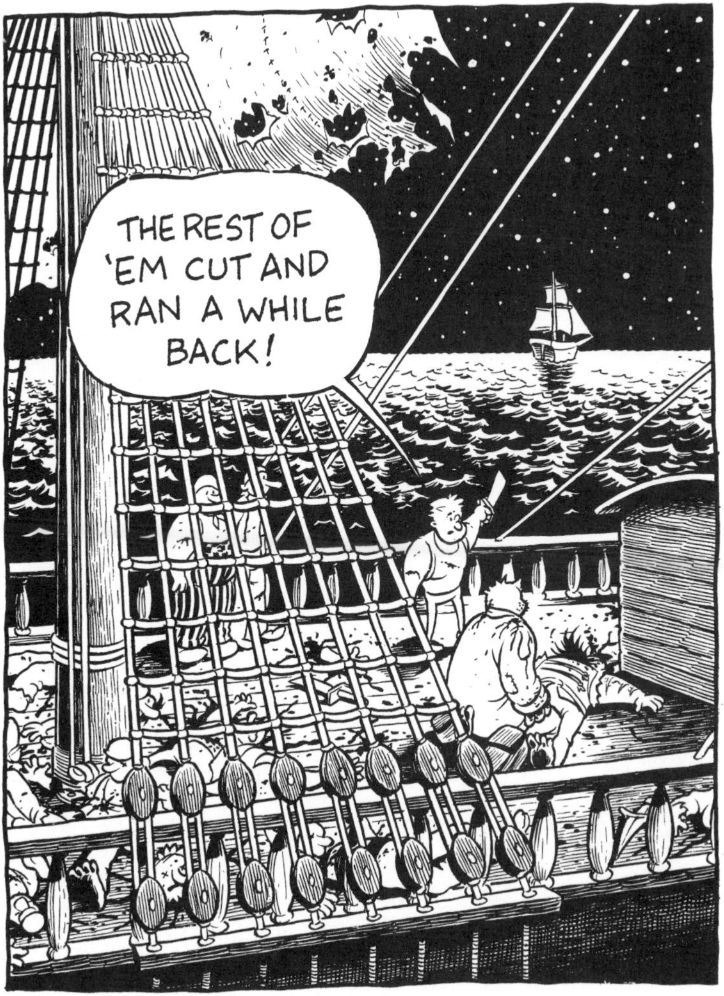
THE REST OF 'EM CUT AND RAN A WHILE BACK!

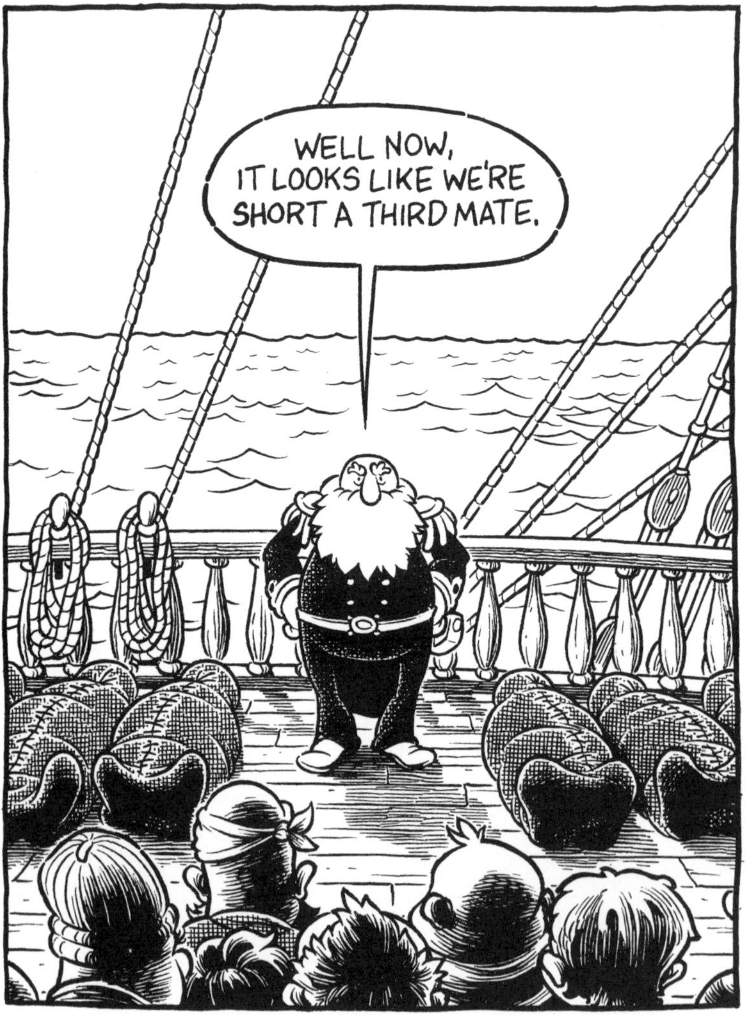
WELL NOW, IT LOOKS LIKE WE'RE SHORT A THIRD MATE.

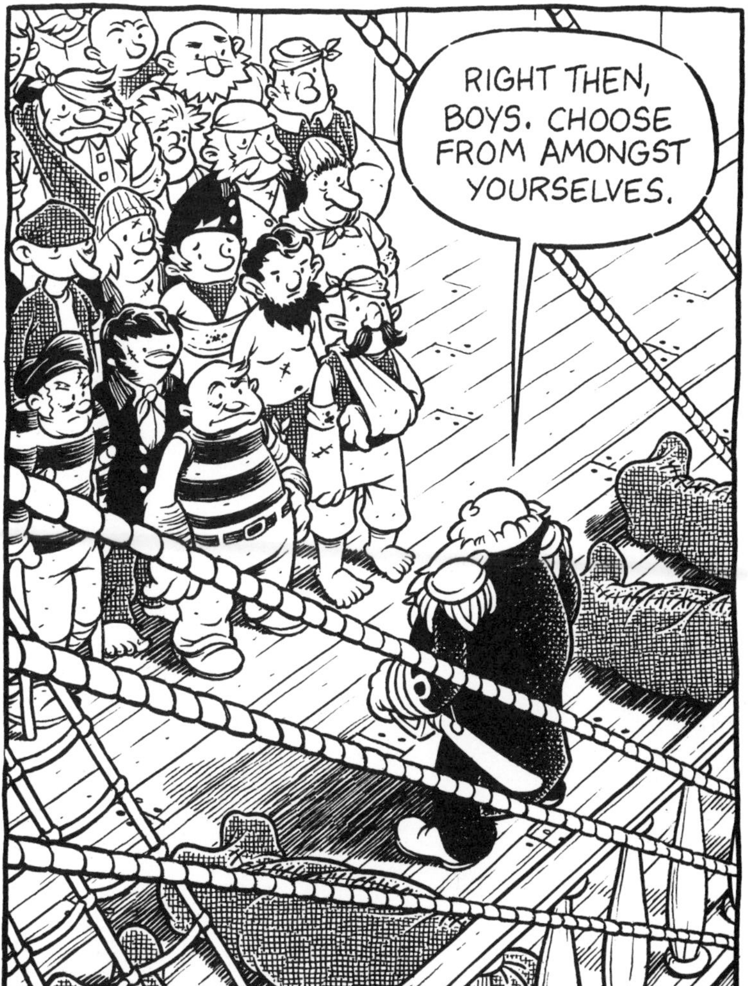
RIGHT THEN, BOYS. CHOOSE FROM AMONGST YOURSELVES.

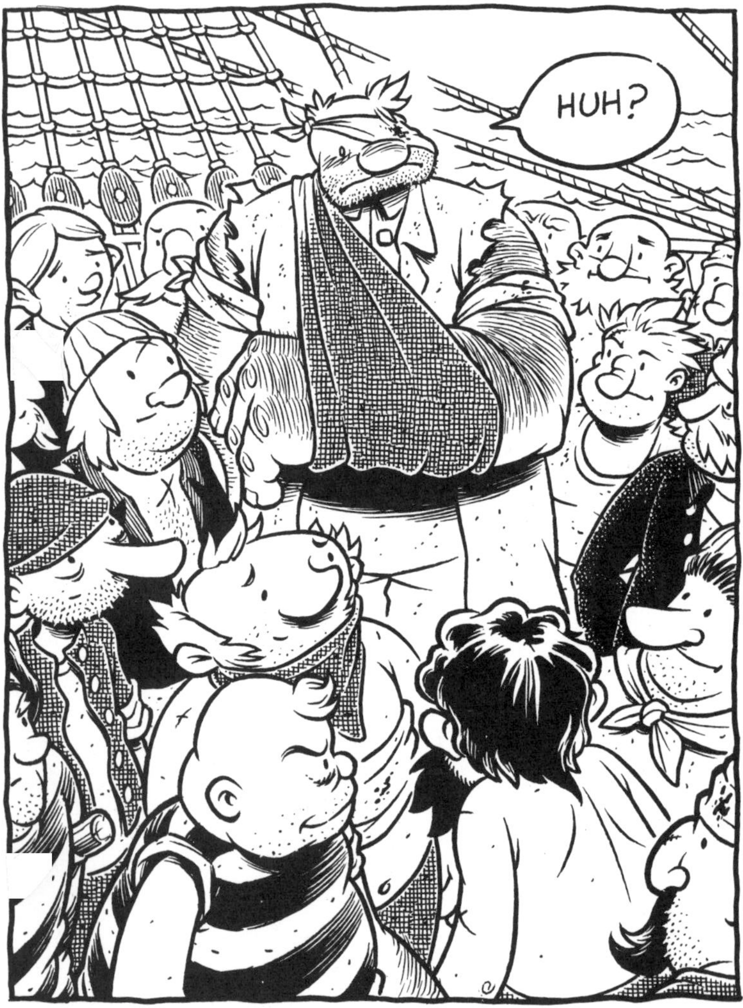
HUH?

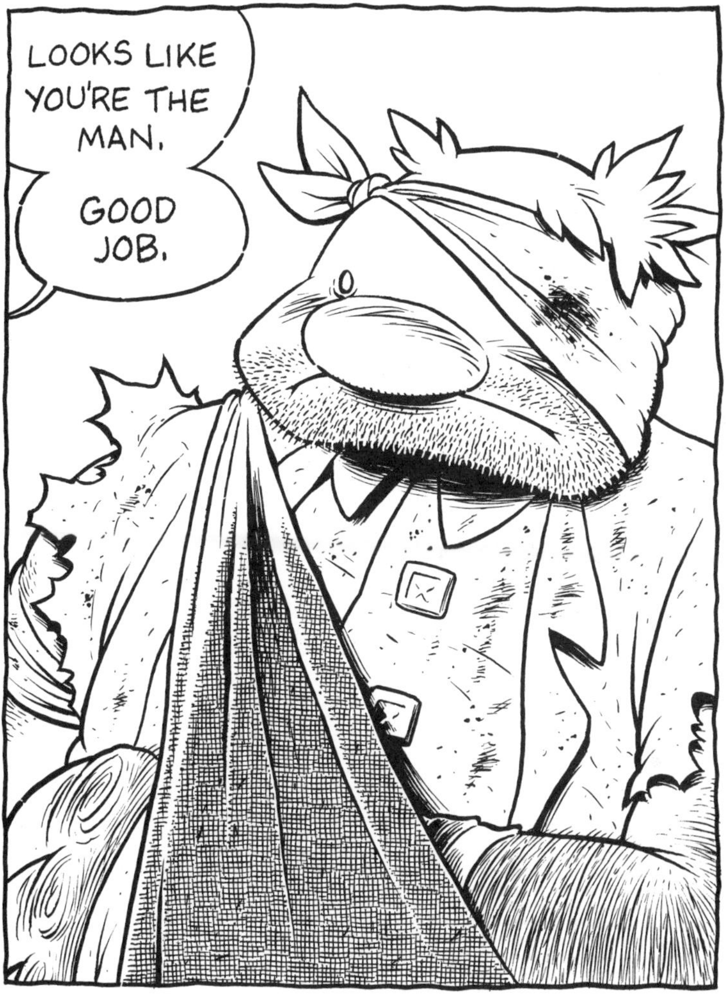
LOOKS LIKE YOU'RE THE MAN.
GOOD JOB.

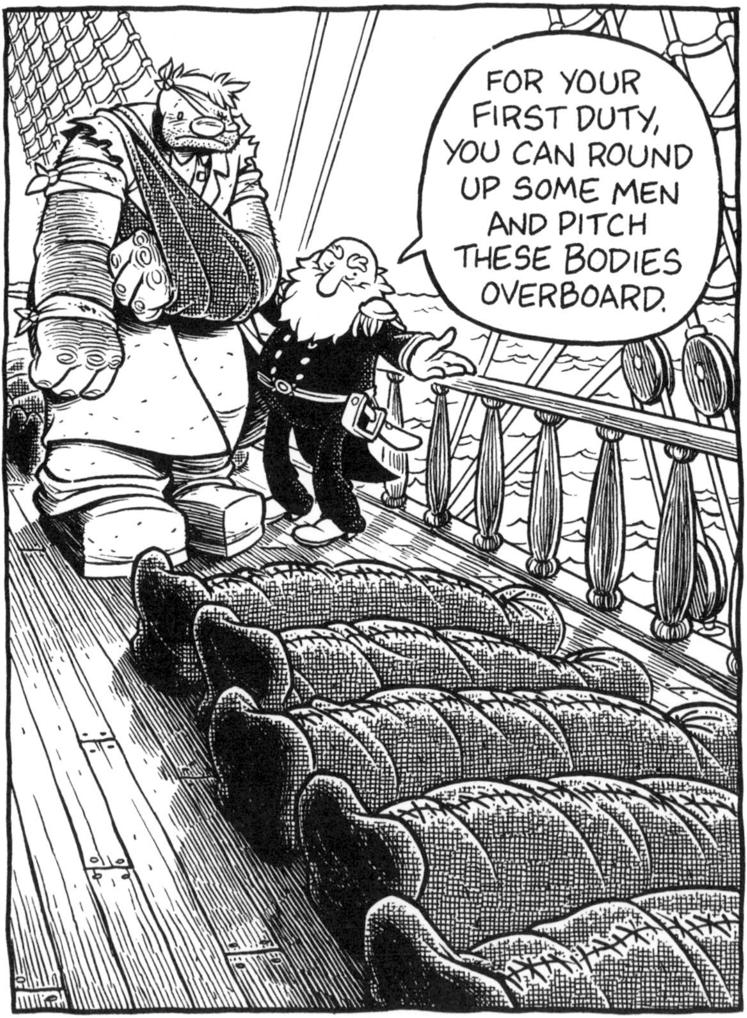
FOR YOUR FIRST DUTY, YOU CAN ROUND UP SOME MEN AND PITCH THESE BODIES OVERBOARD.

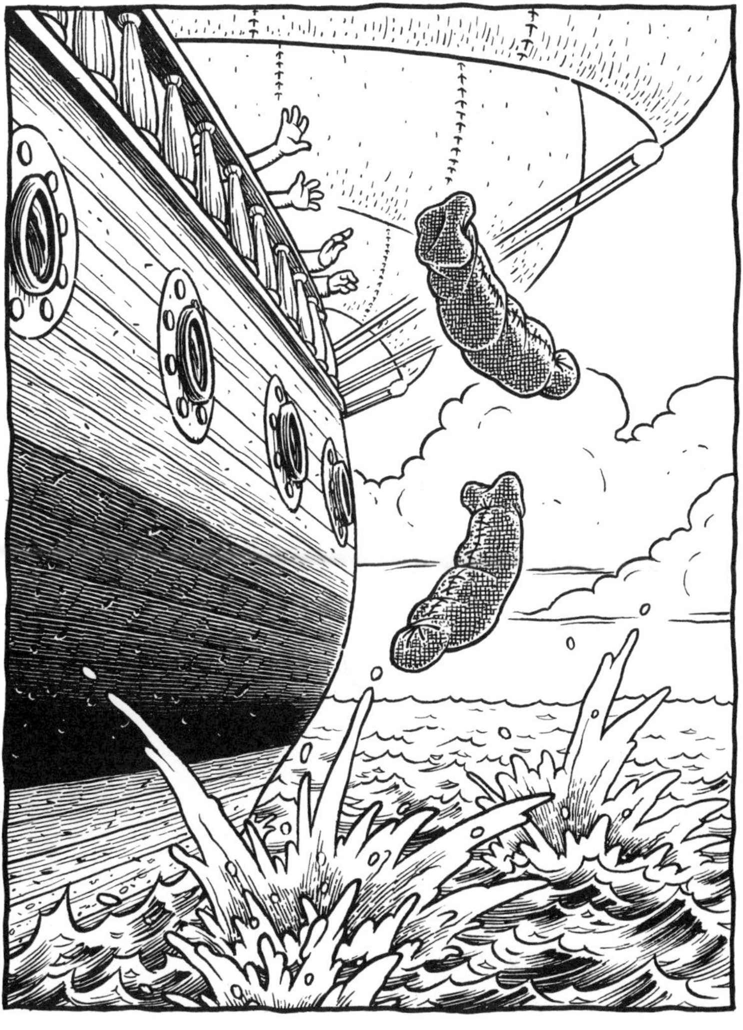

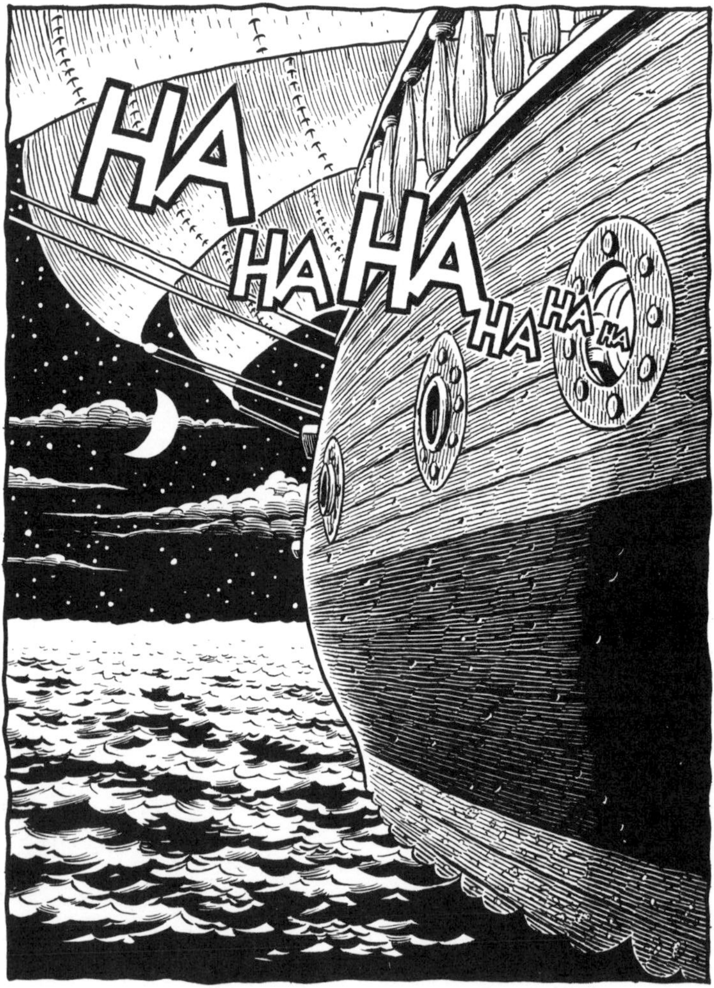
HA HA HA HA HA HA HA

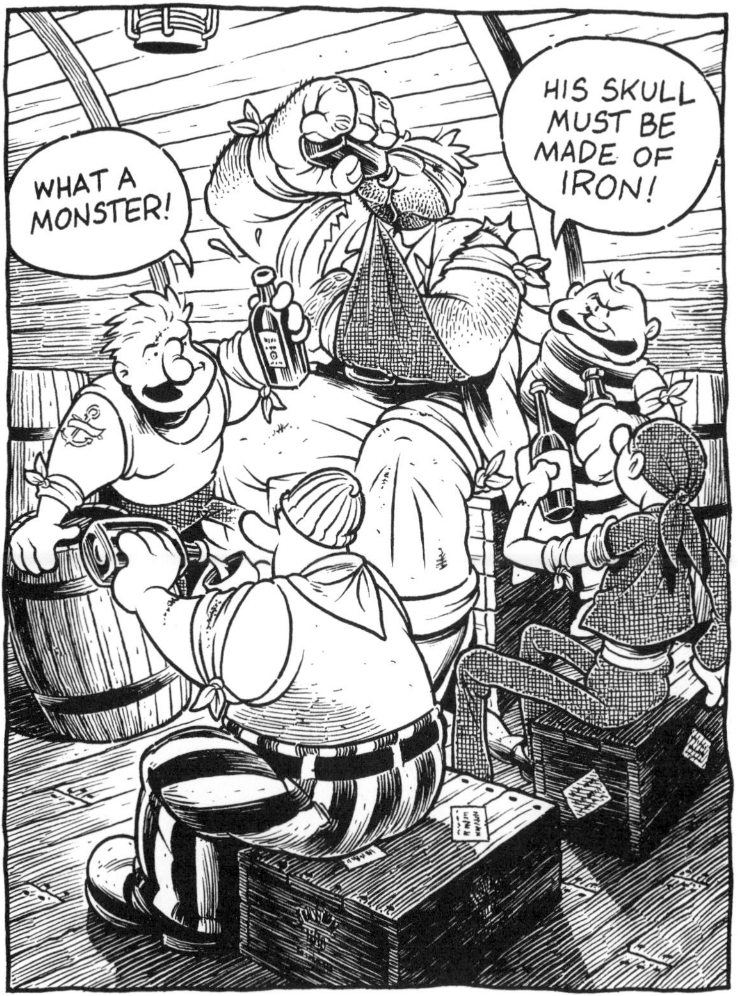
WHAT A MONSTER!
HIS SKULL MUST BE MADE OF IRON!

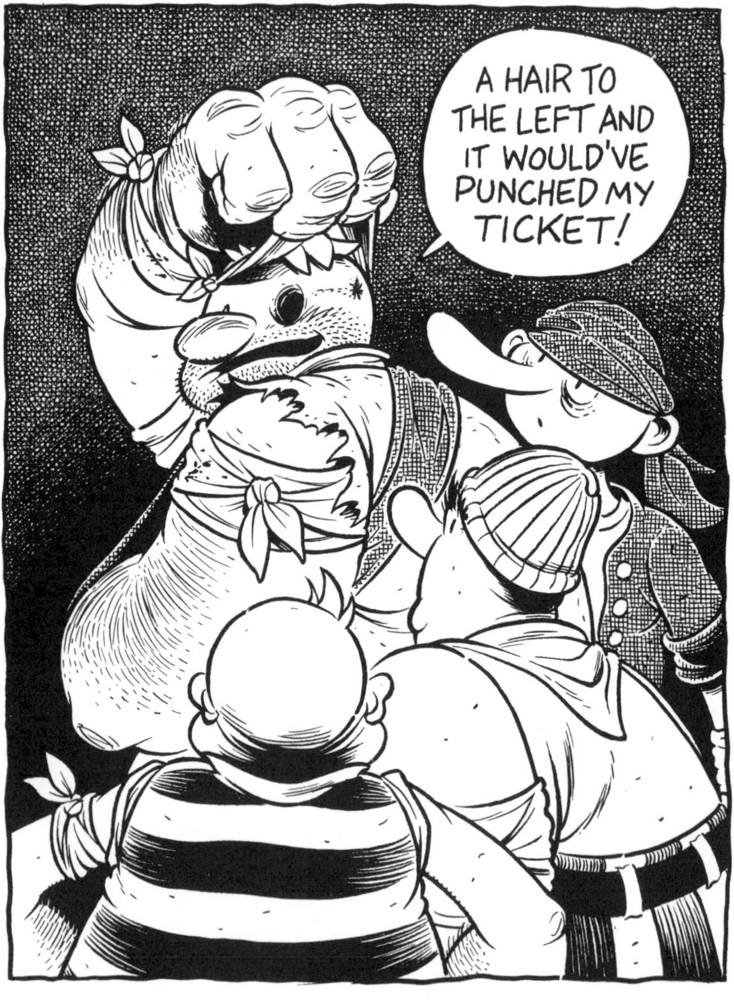
A HAIR TO THE LEFT AND IT WOULD'VE PUNCHED MY TICKET!

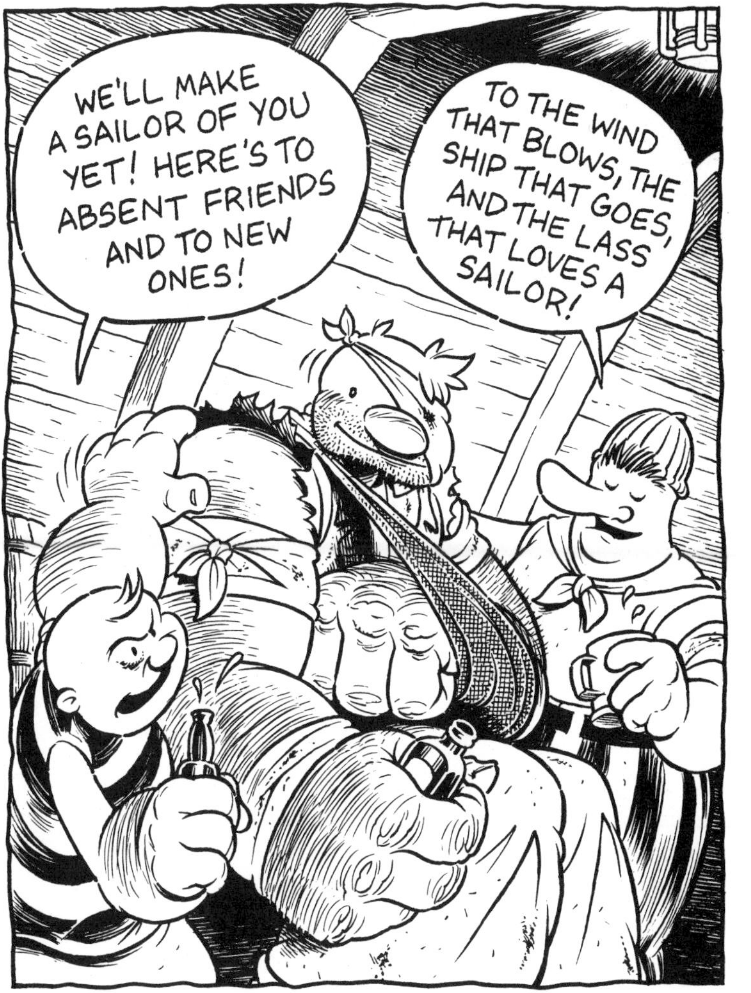
WE'LL MAKE A SAILOR OF YOU YET! HERE'S TO ABSENT FRIENDS AND TO NEW ONES!
TO THE WIND THAT BLOWS, THE SHIP THAT GOES, AND THE LASS THAT LOVES A SAILOR!

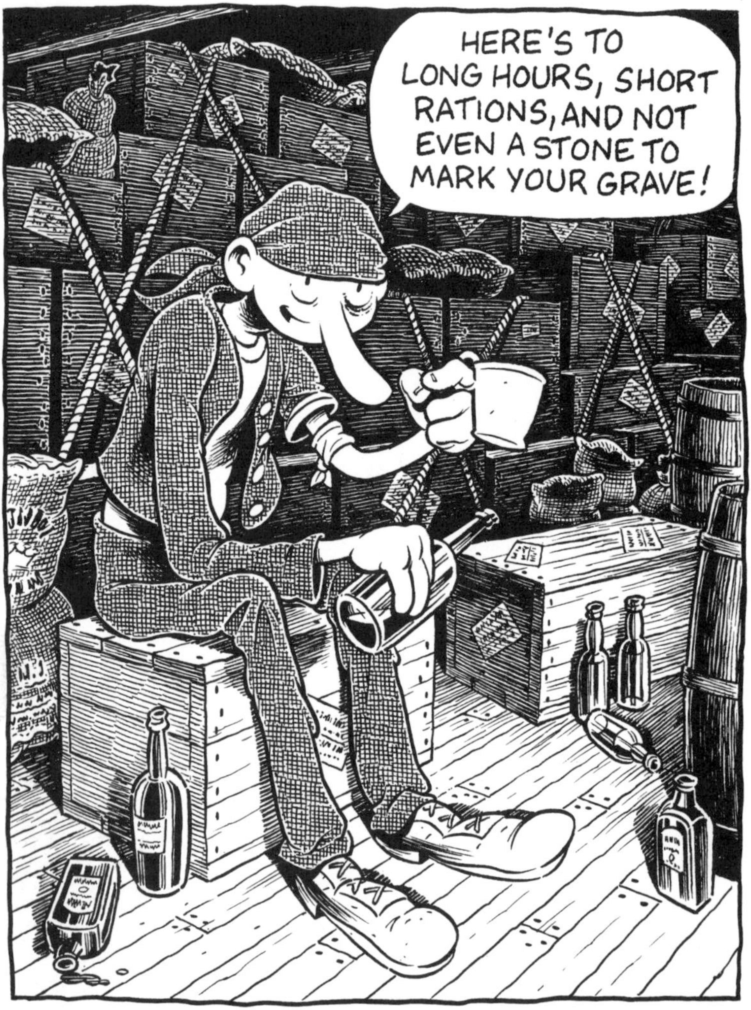
HERE'S TO LONG HOURS, SHORT RATIONS, AND NOT EVEN A STONE TO MARK YOUR GRAVE!

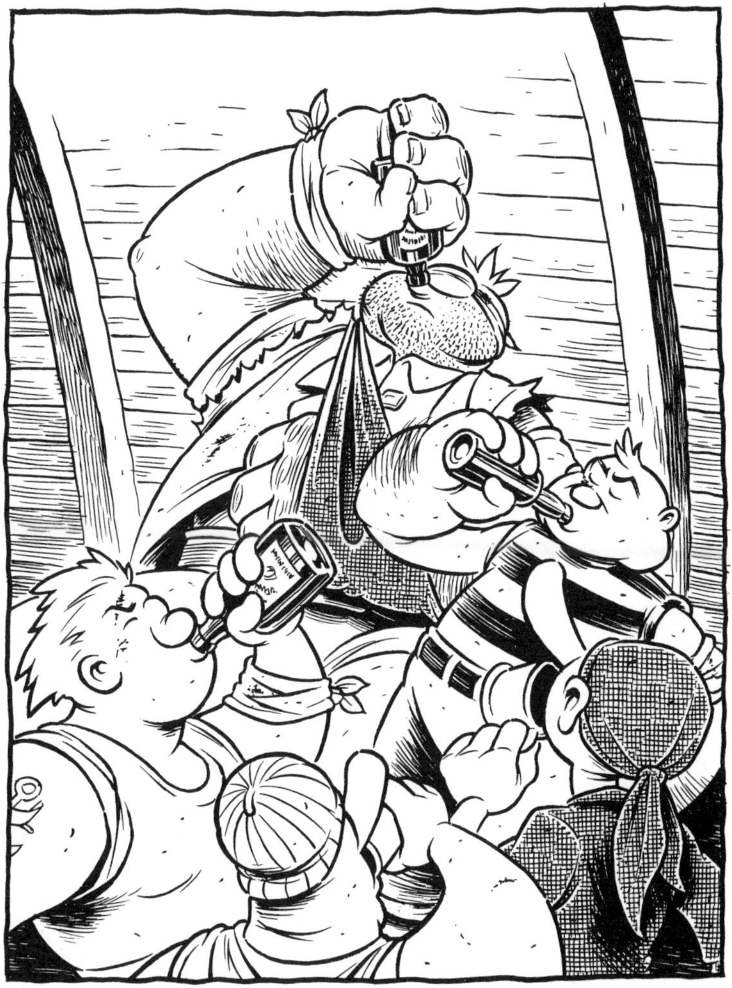

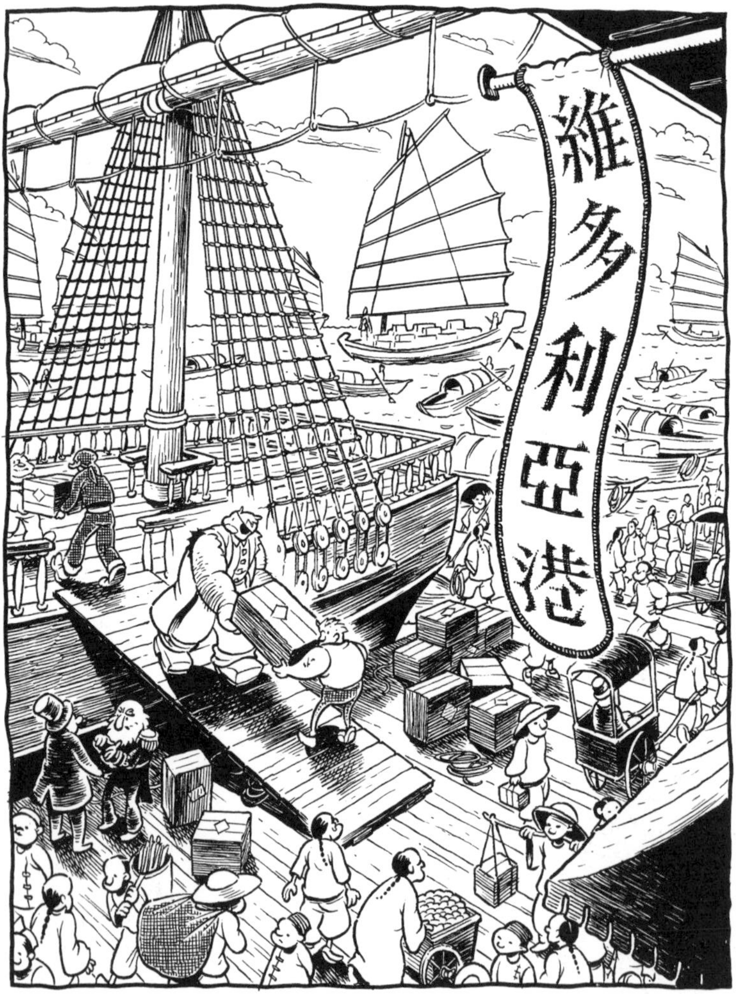
維多利亞港

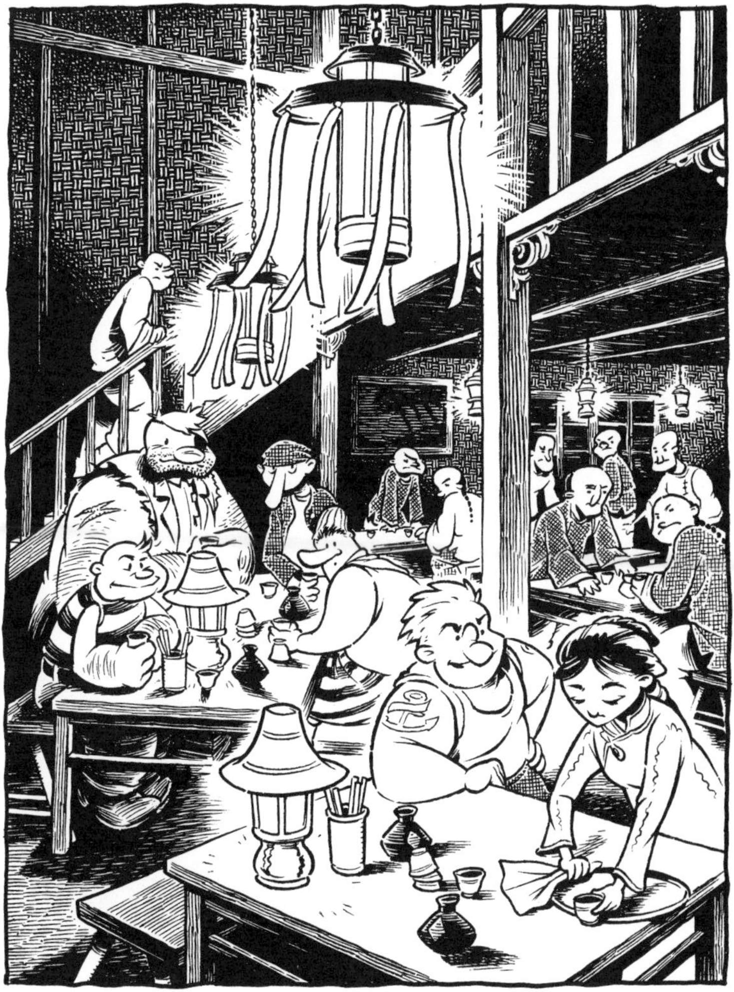

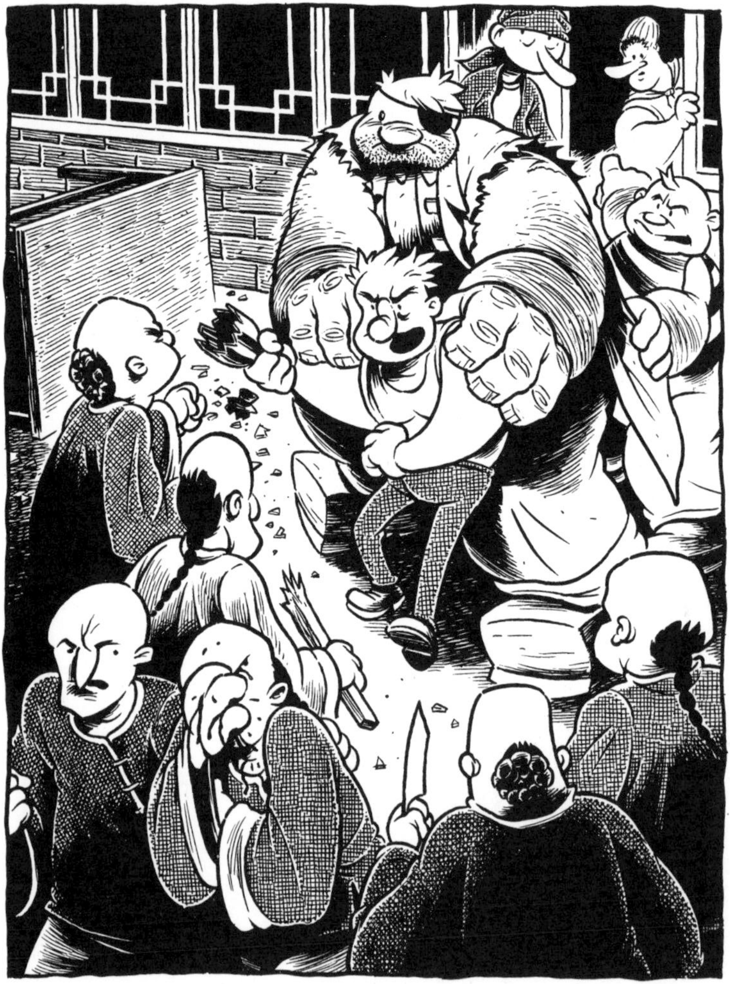

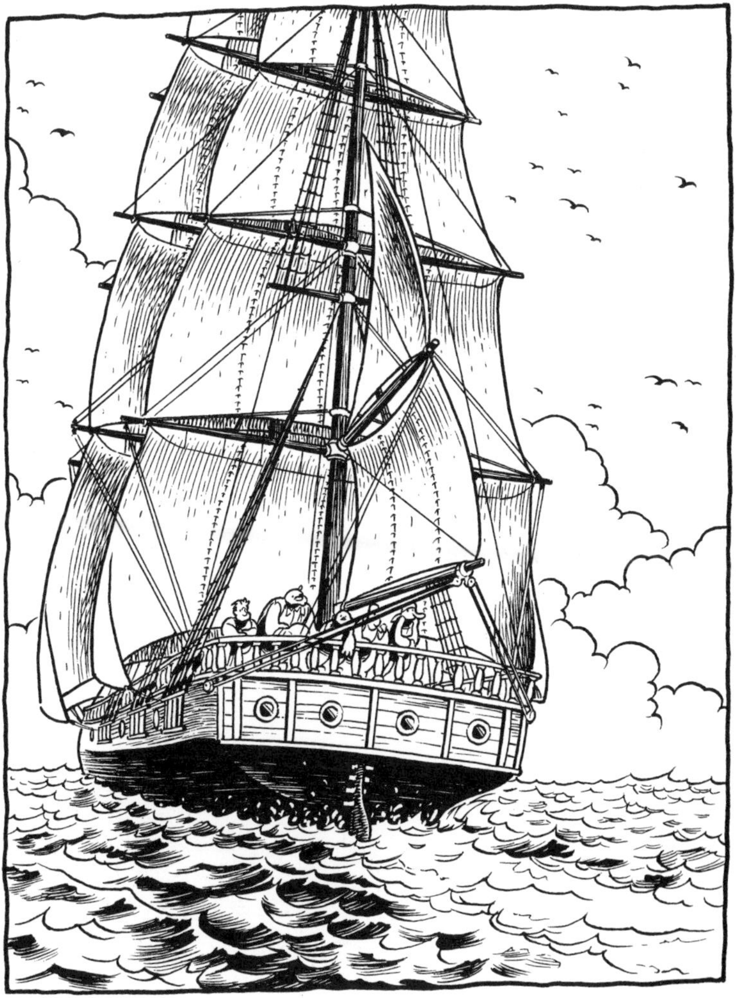

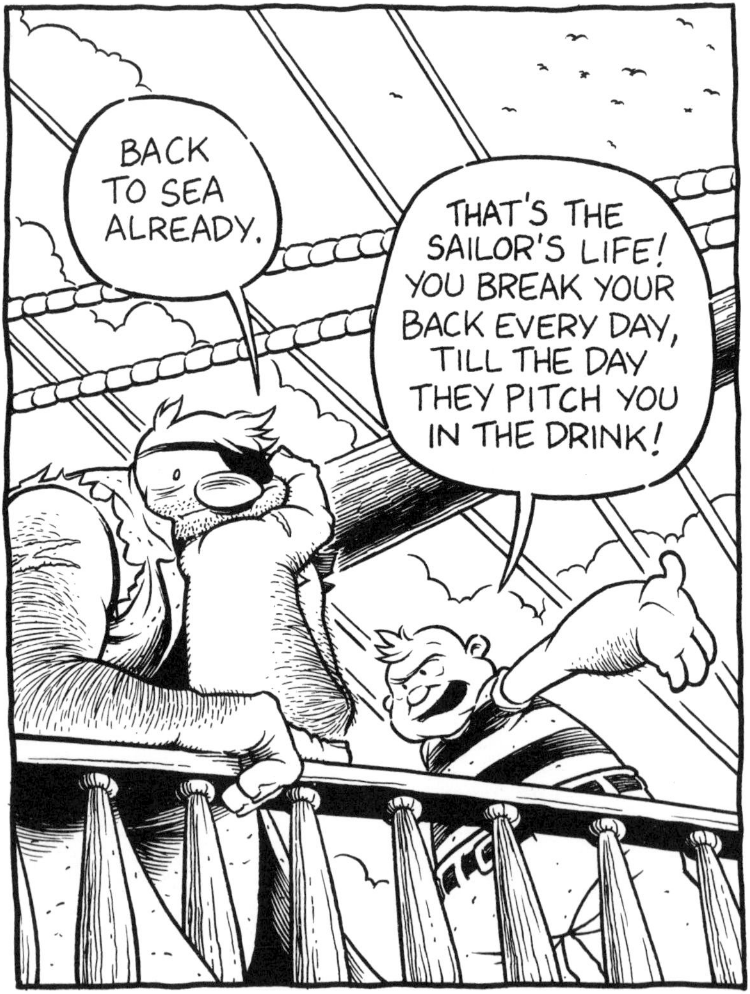
BACK TO SEA ALREADY.
THAT'S THE SAILOR'S LIFE! YOU BREAK YOUR BACK EVERY DAY, TILL THE DAY THEY PITCH YOU IN THE DRINK!

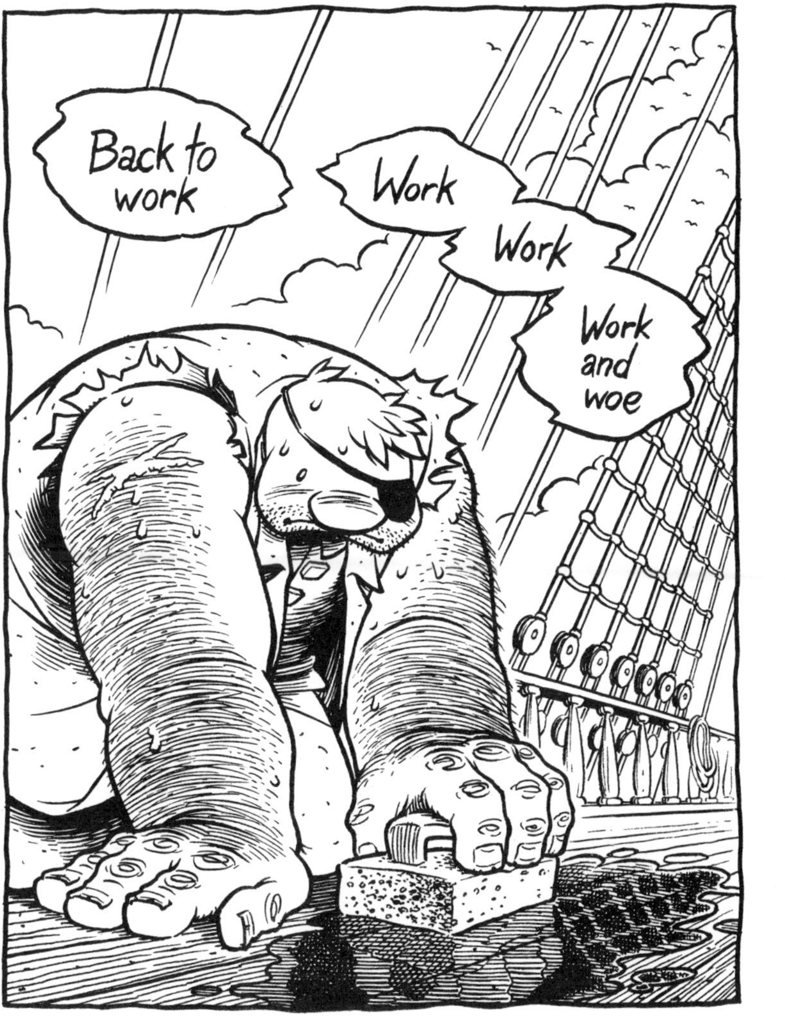
Back to work
Work
Work
Work and woe

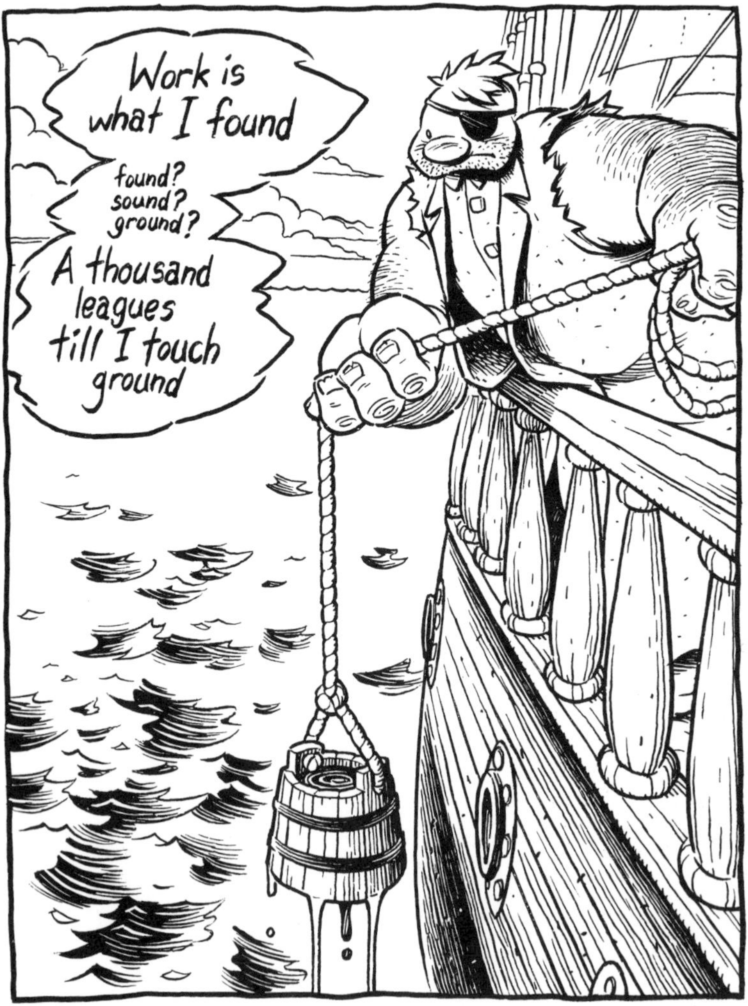
Work is what I found
found? sound? ground?
A thousand leagues till I touch ground

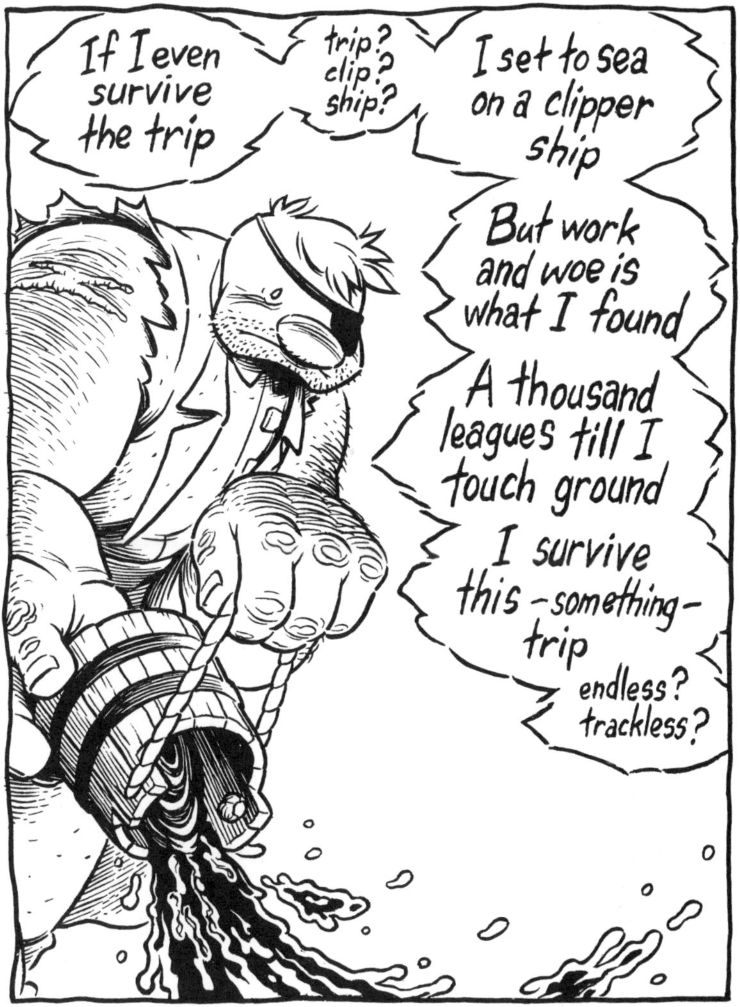
If I even survive the trip
trip? clip? ship?
I set to sea on a clipper ship
But work and woe is what I found
A thousand leagues till I touch ground
I survive this -something- trip
endless? trackless?

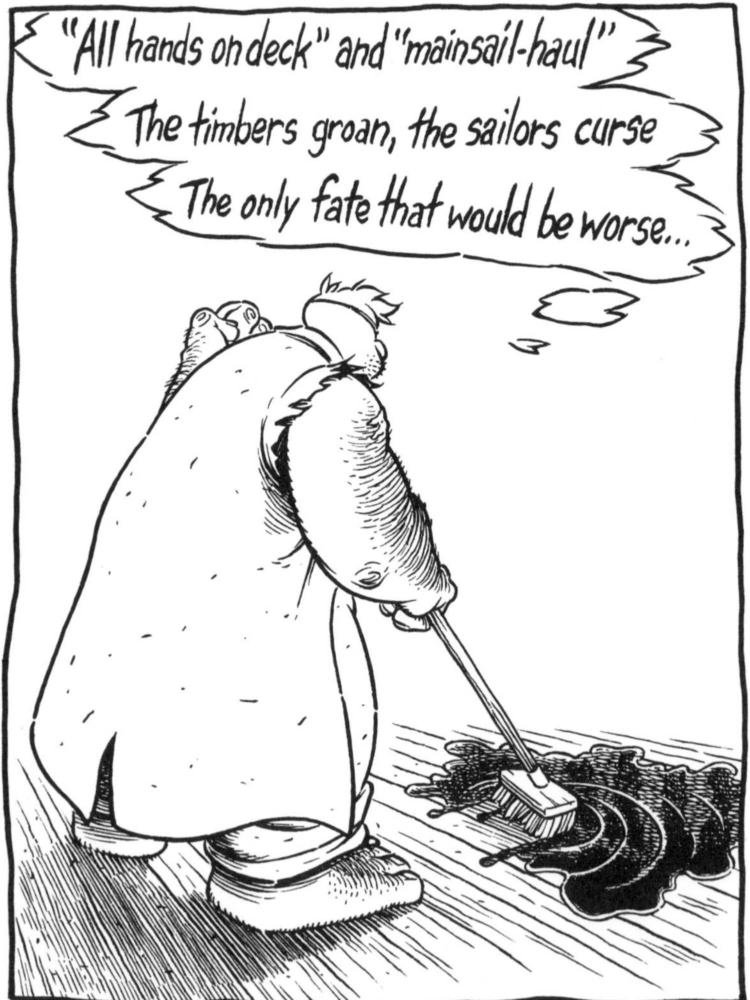
"All hands on deck" and "mainsail-haul"
The timbers groan, the sailors curse
The only fate that would be worse...

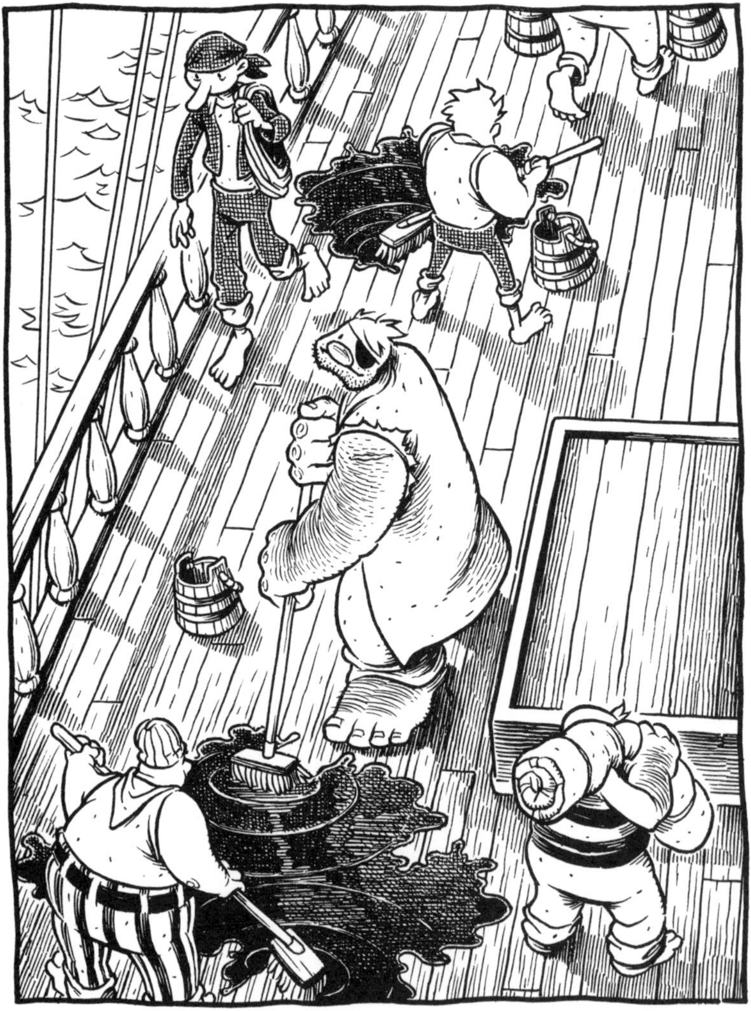

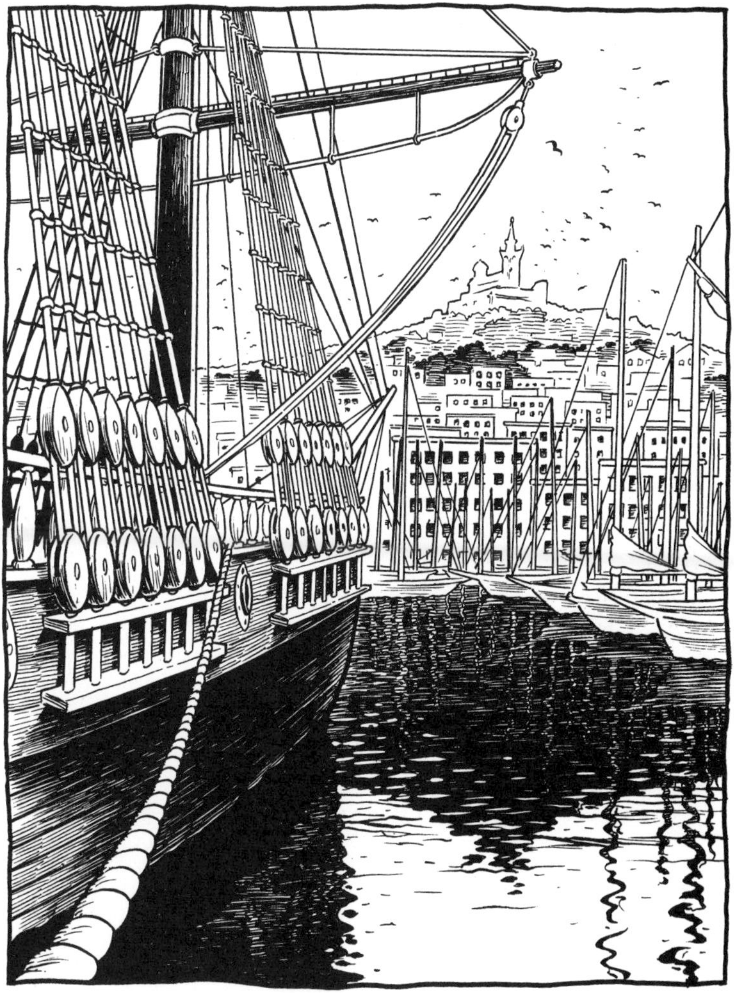

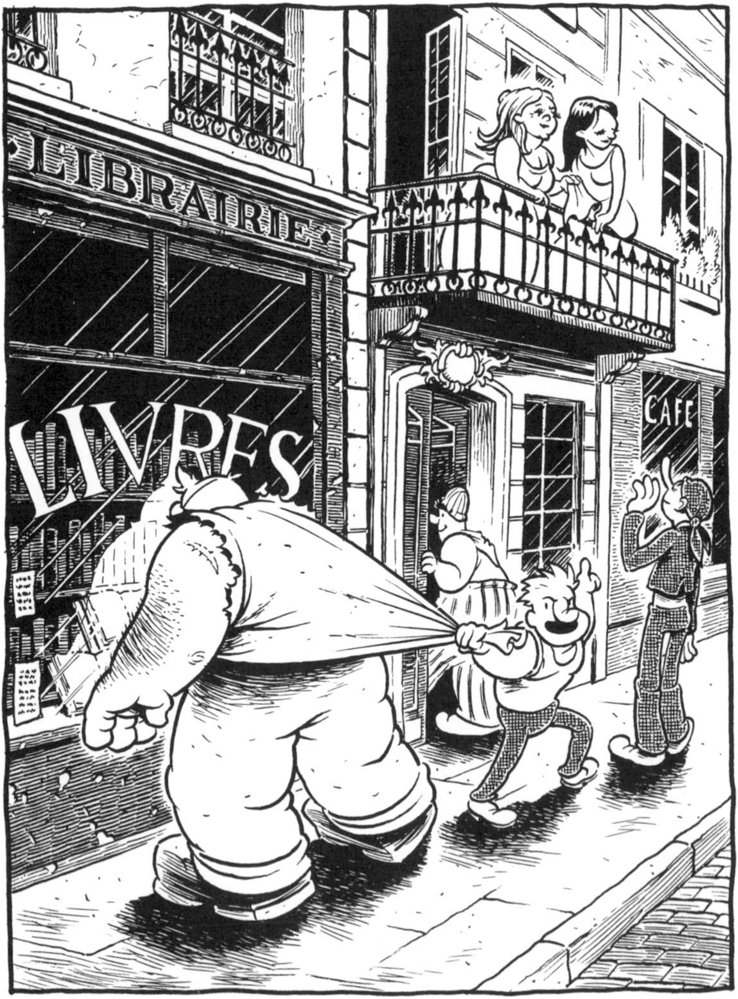
L'IBRAIRIE
LIVRES
CAFE

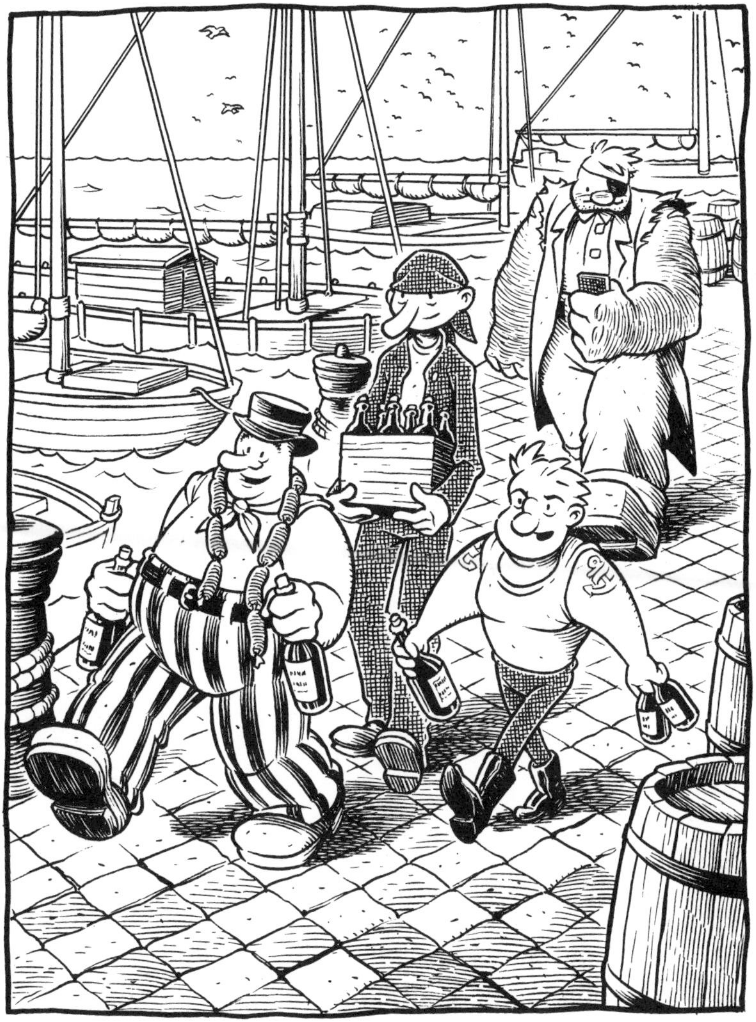

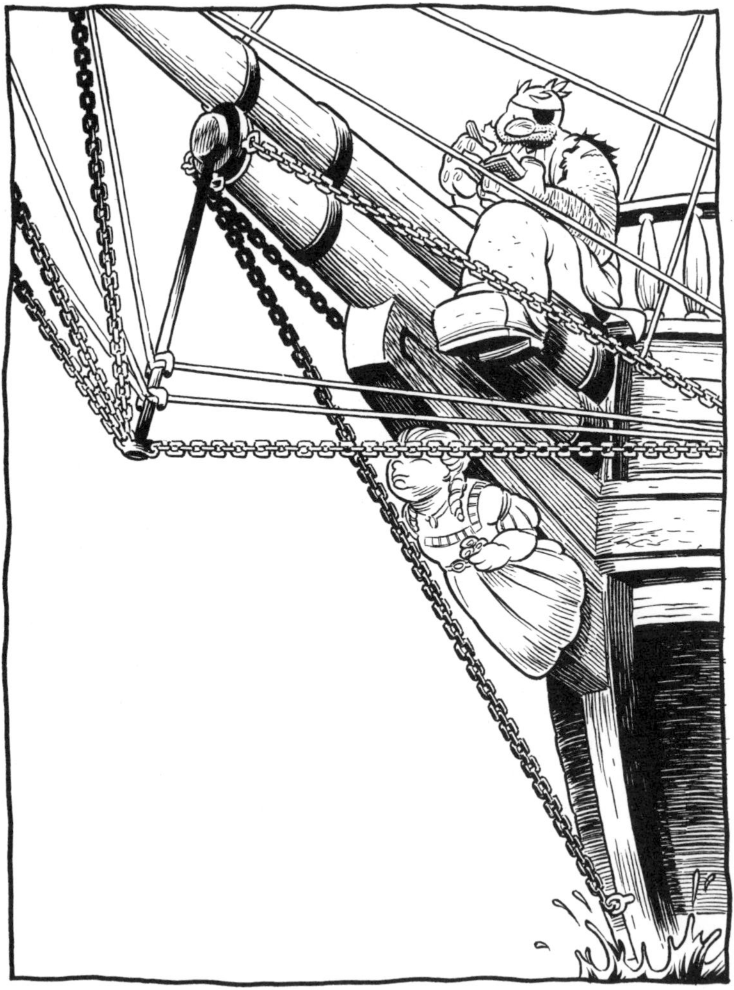

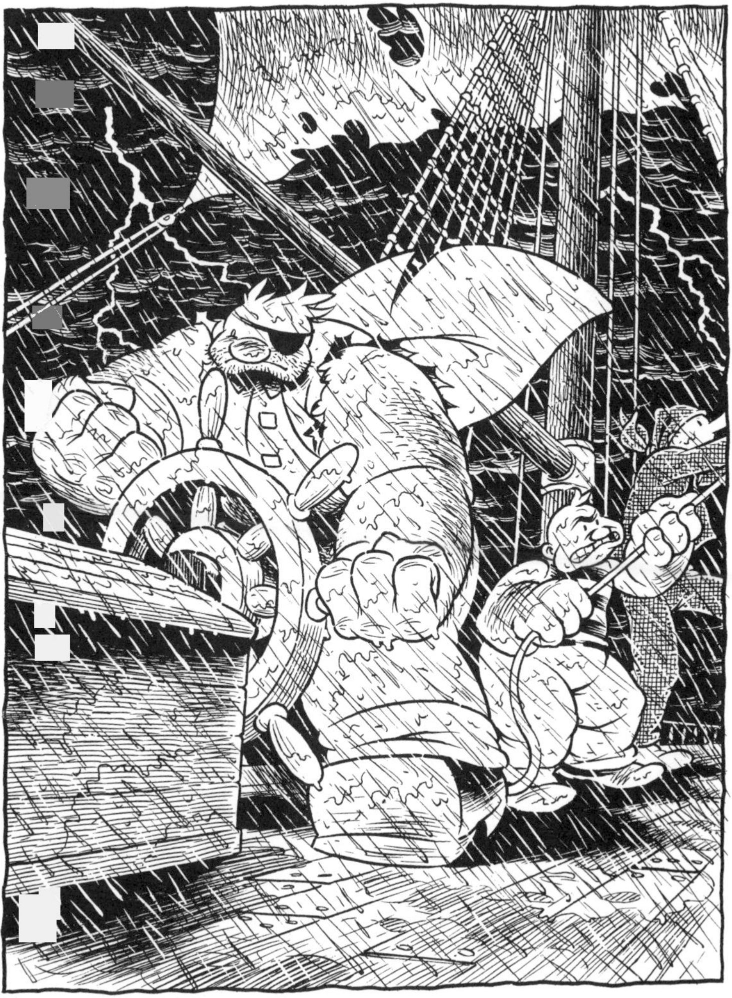

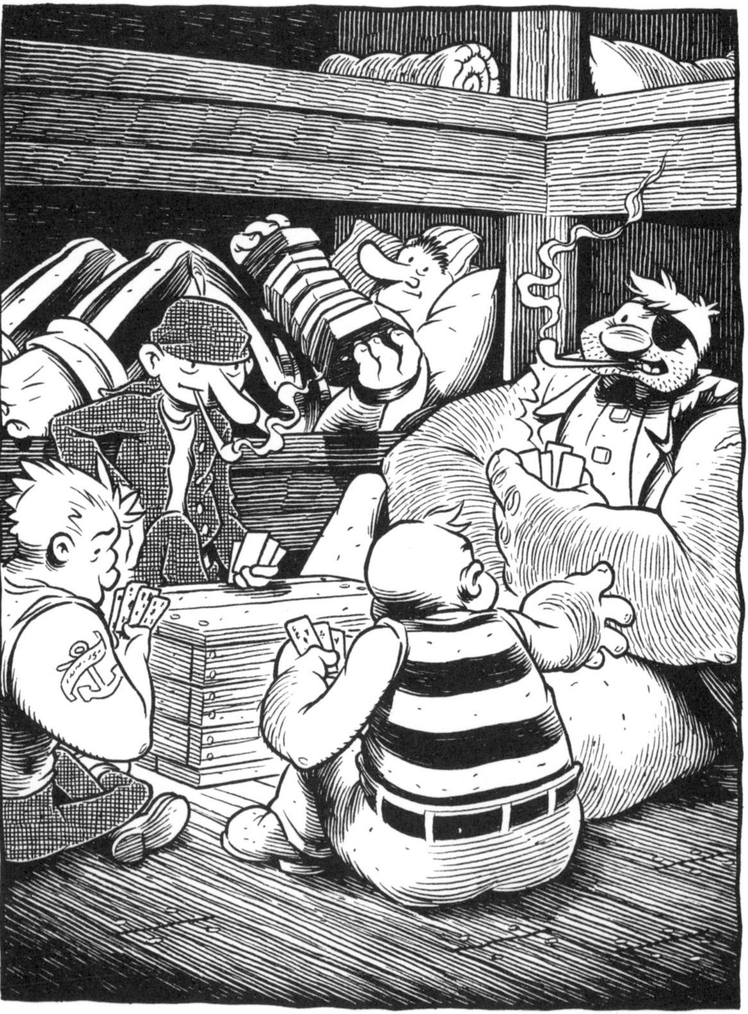

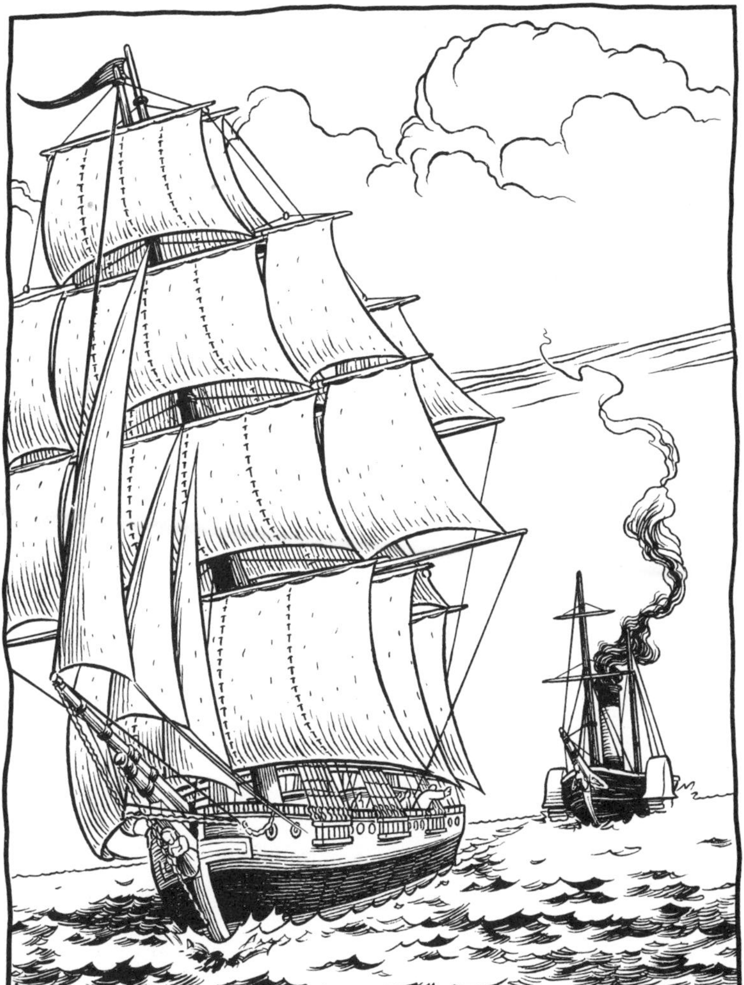

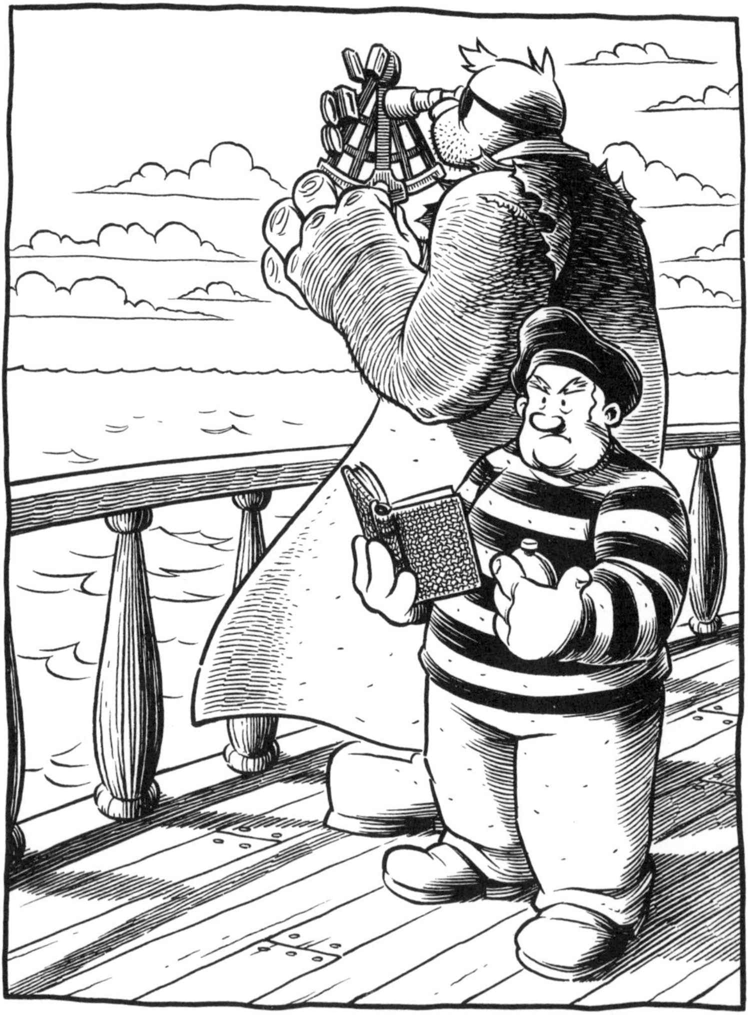

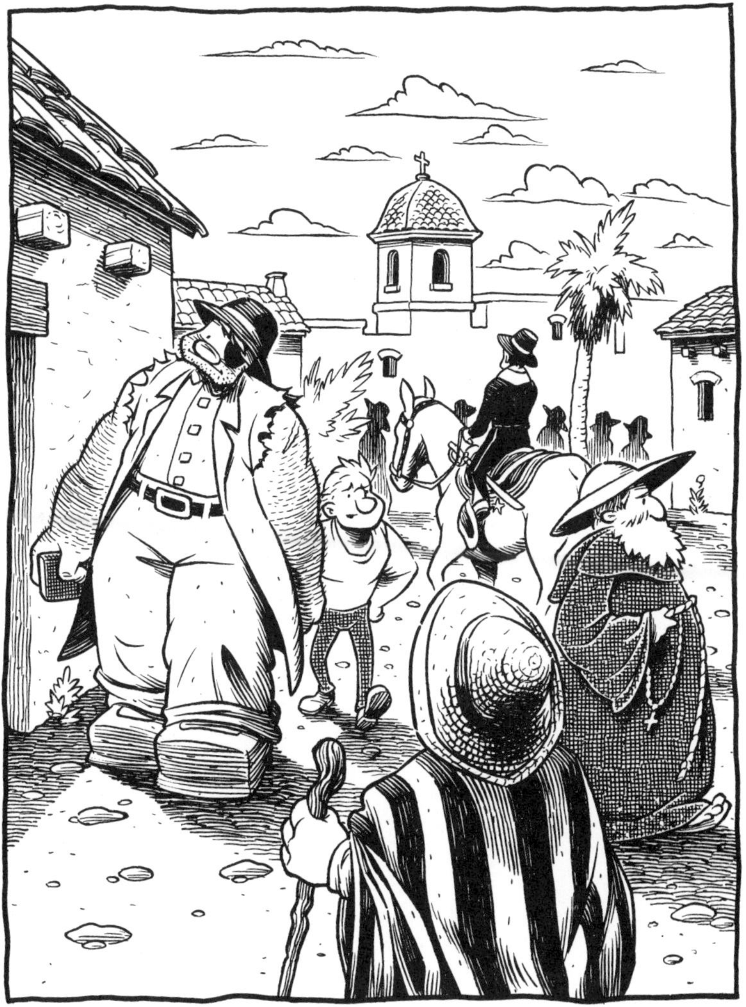

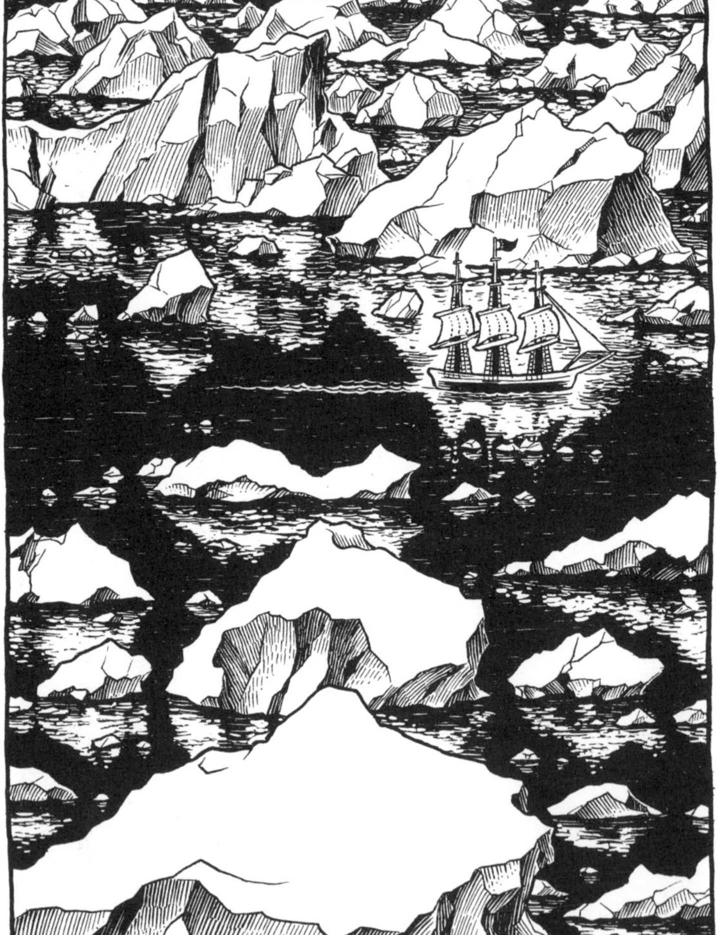

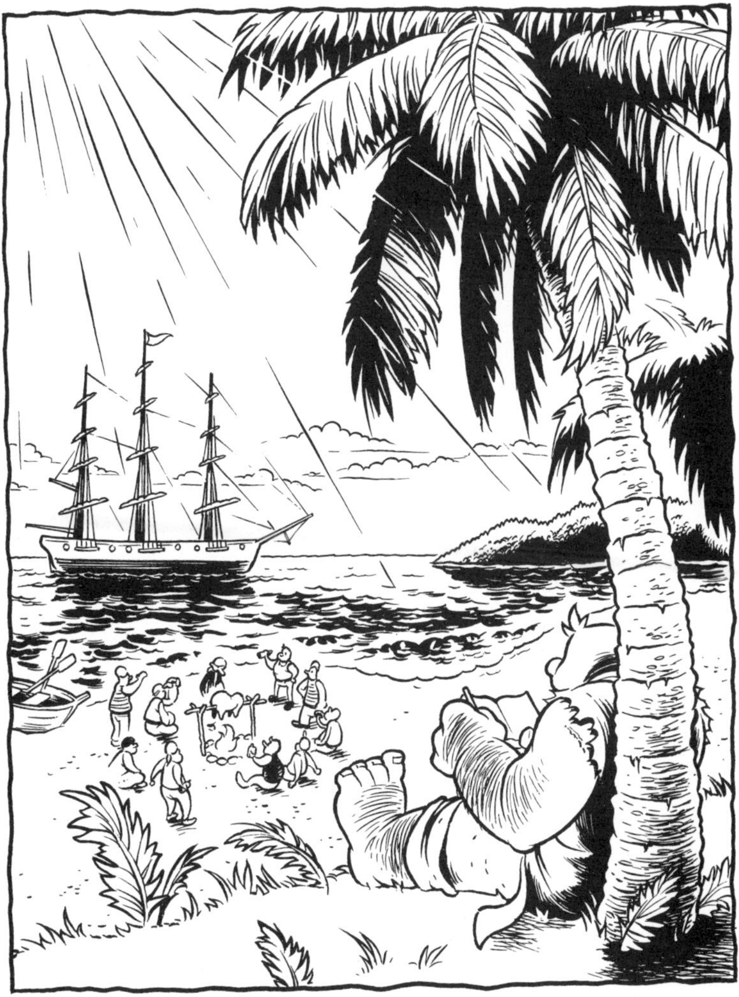

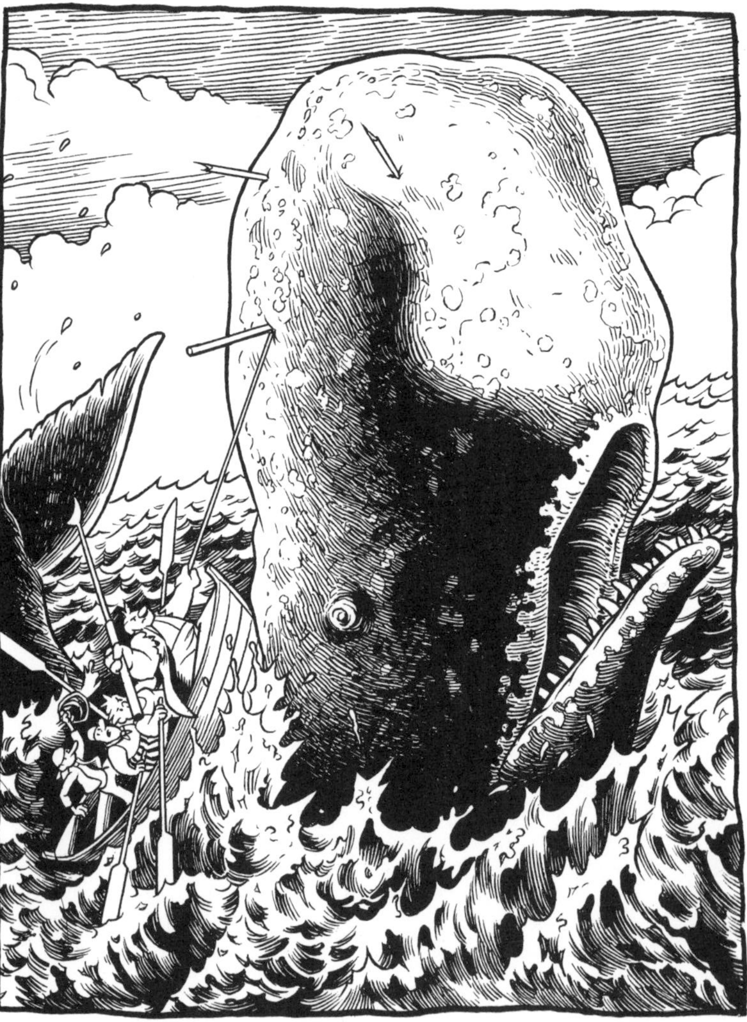

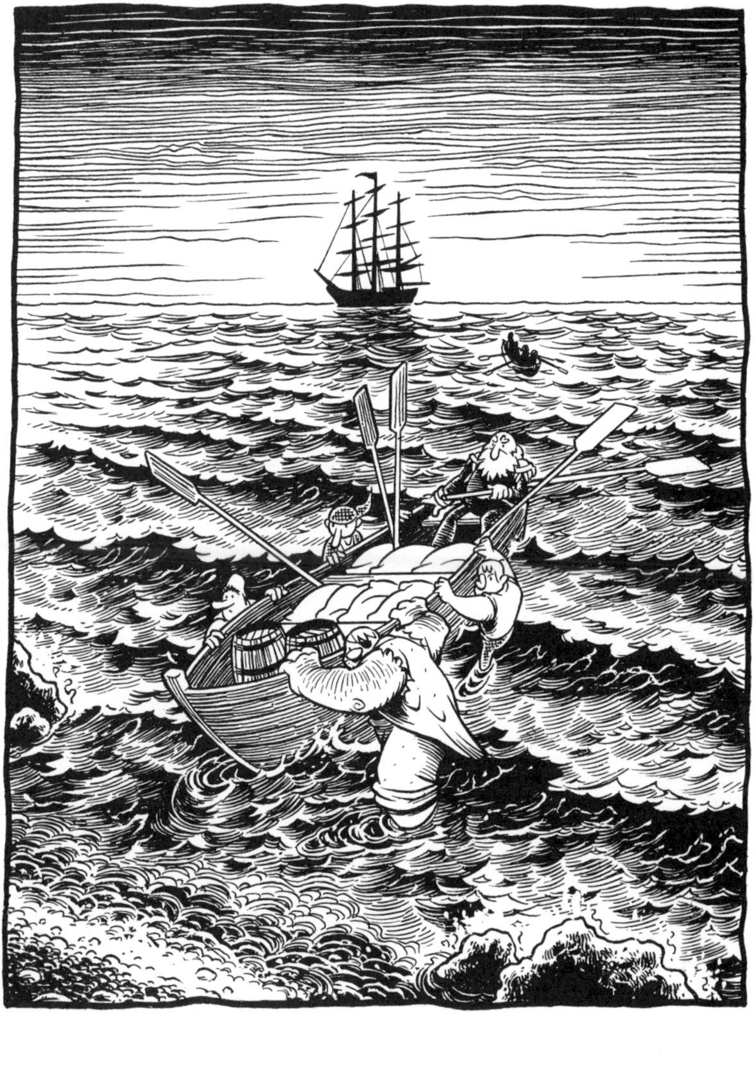

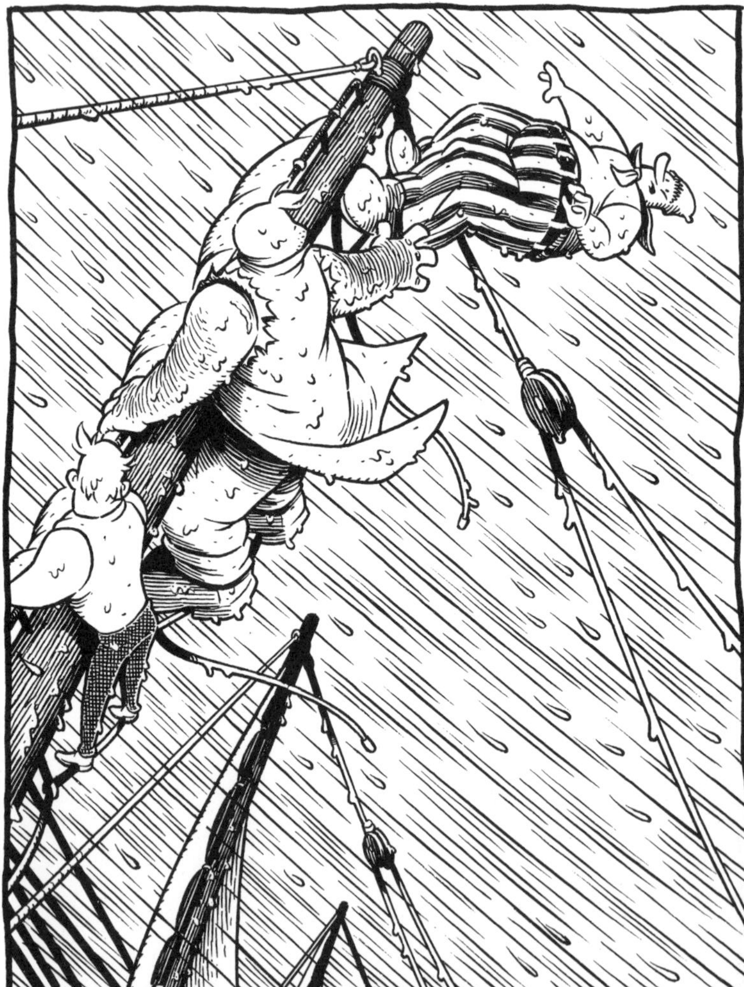

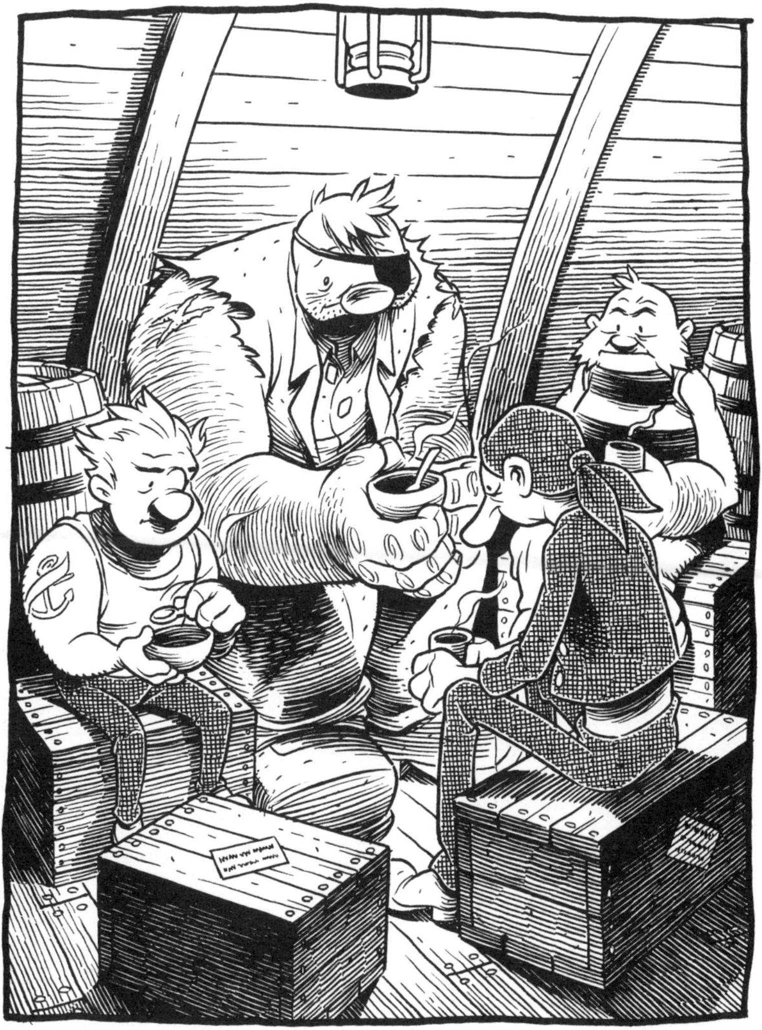

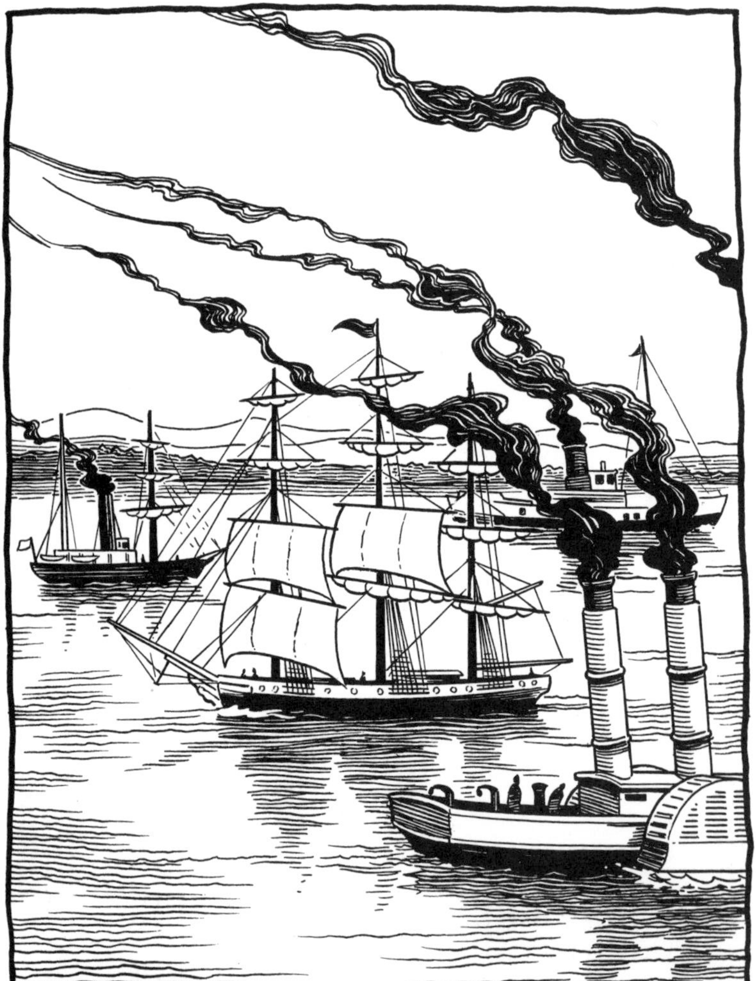

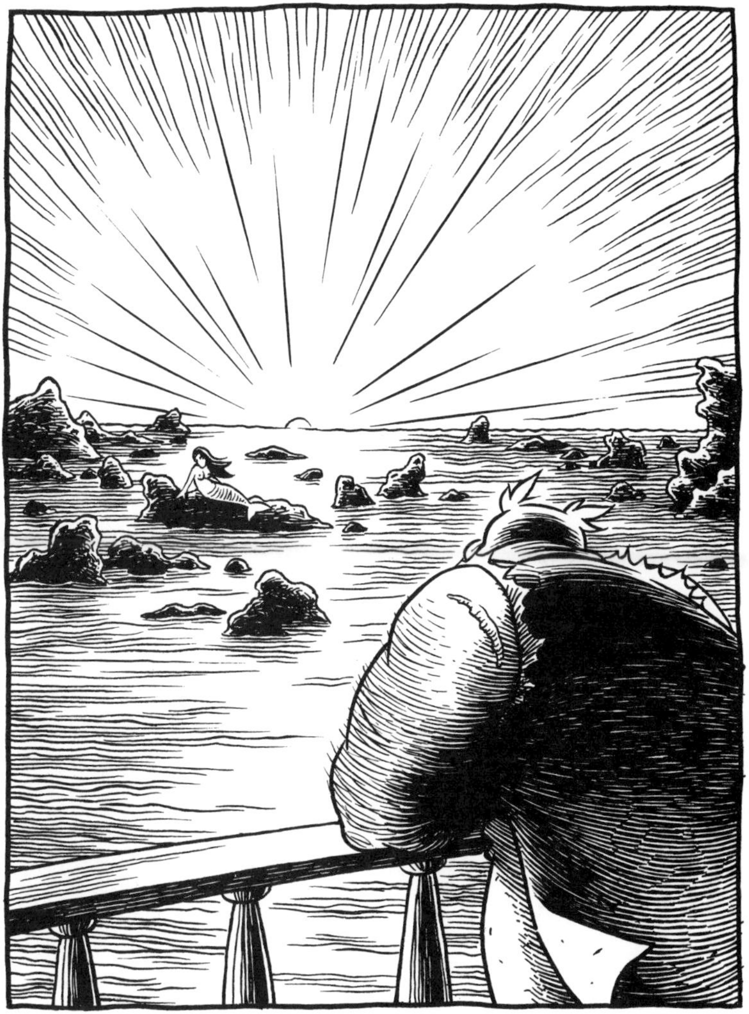

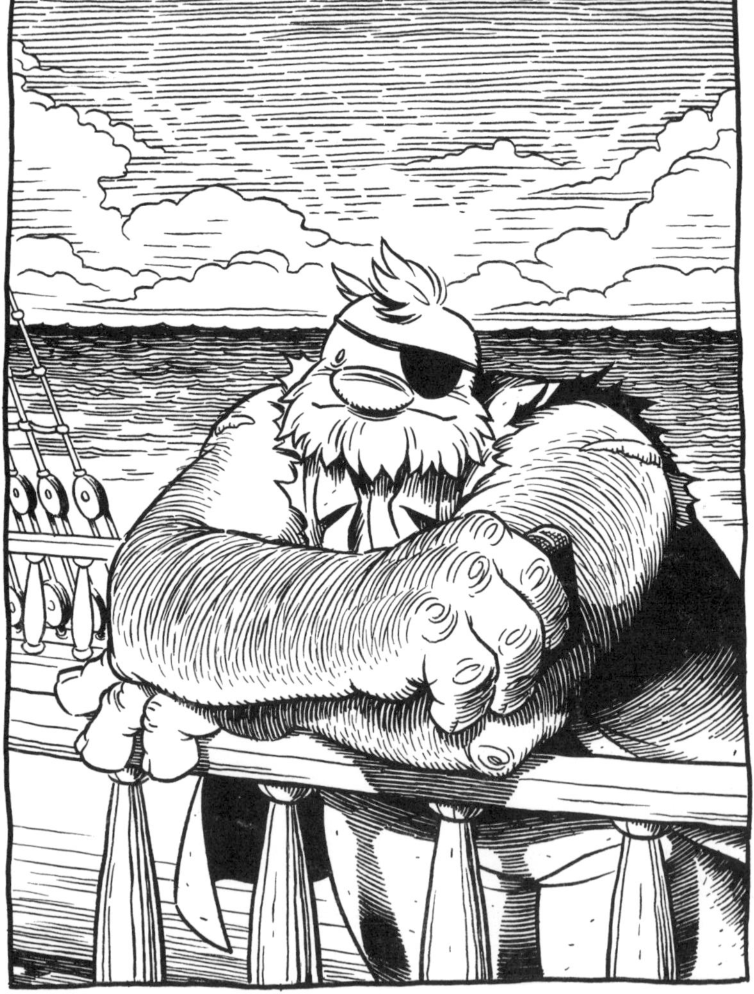

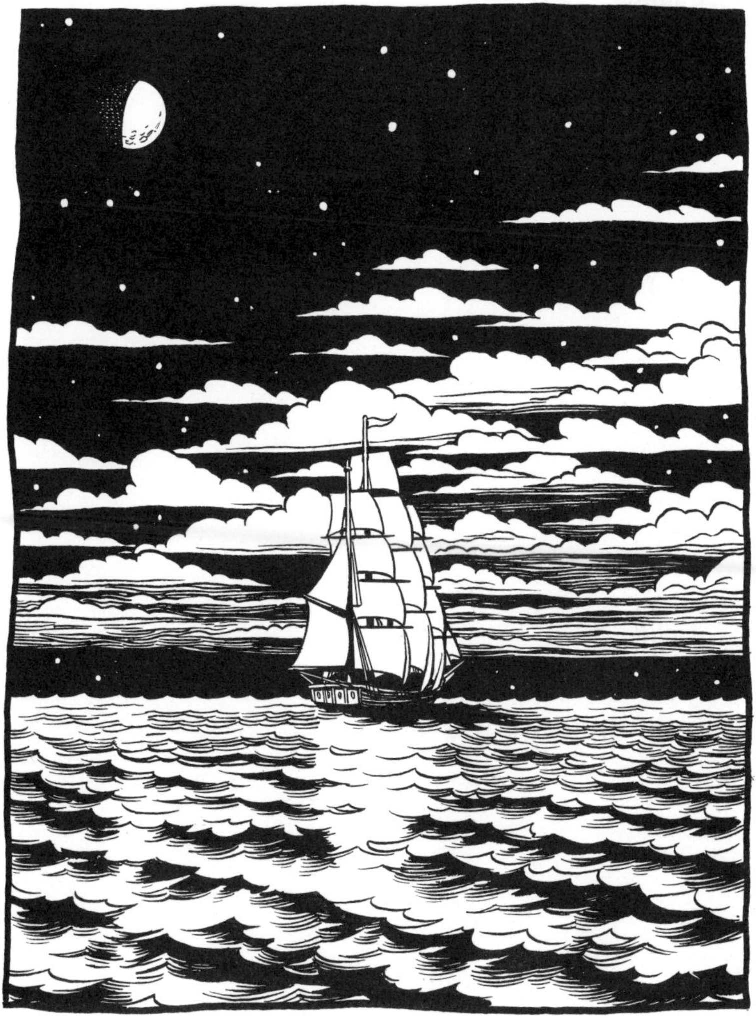

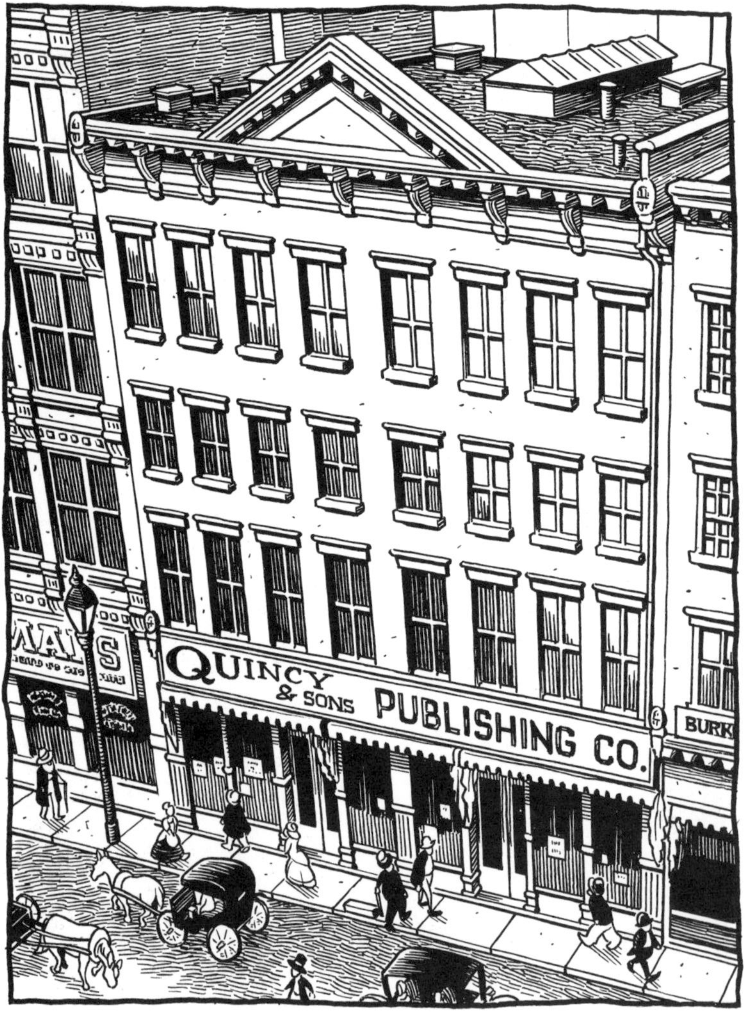
QUINCY
& SONS
PUBLISHING CO.
BURK

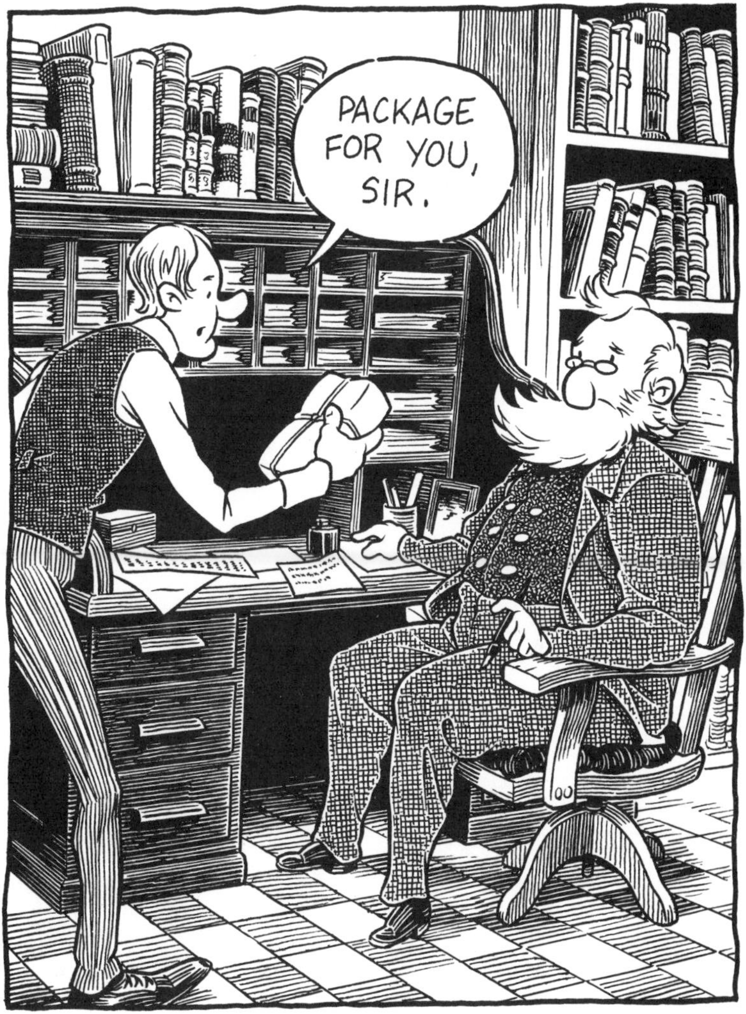
PACKAGE FOR YOU, SIR.

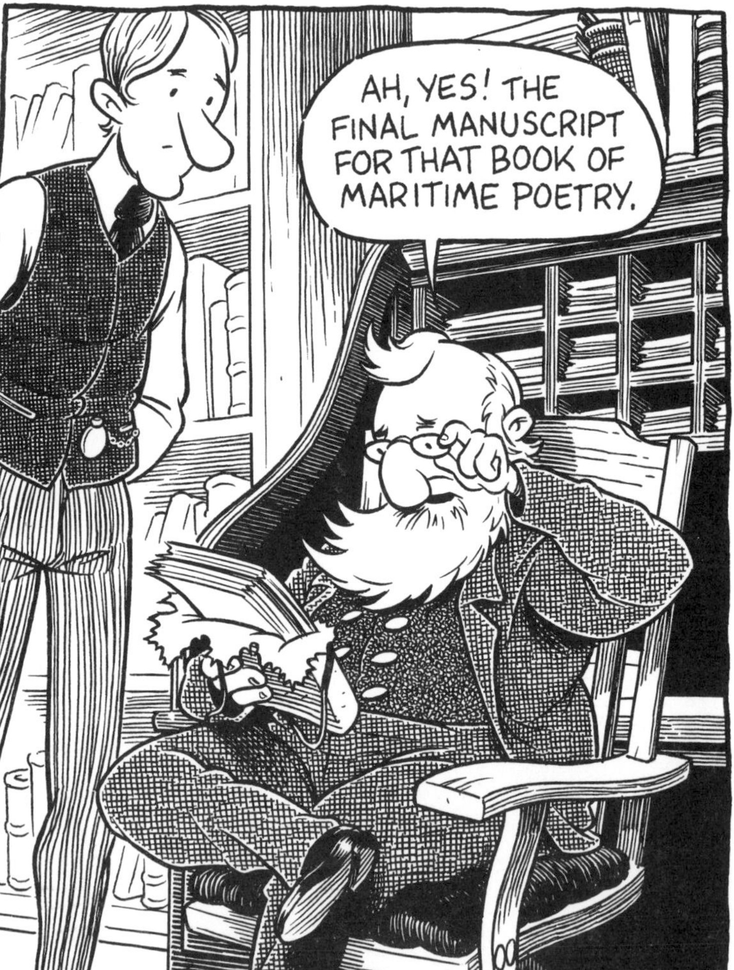
AH, YES! THE FINAL MANUSCRIPT FOR THAT BOOK OF MARITIME POETRY.

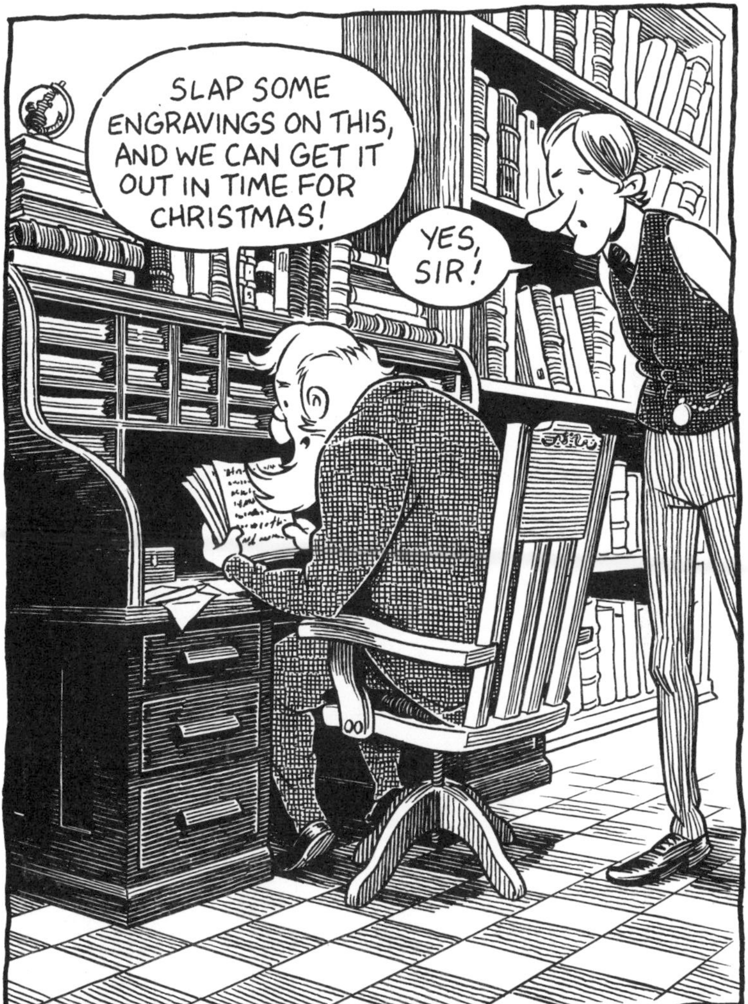
SLAP SOME ENGRAVINGS ON THIS, AND WE CAN GET IT OUT IN TIME FOR CHRISTMAS!
YES, SIR!

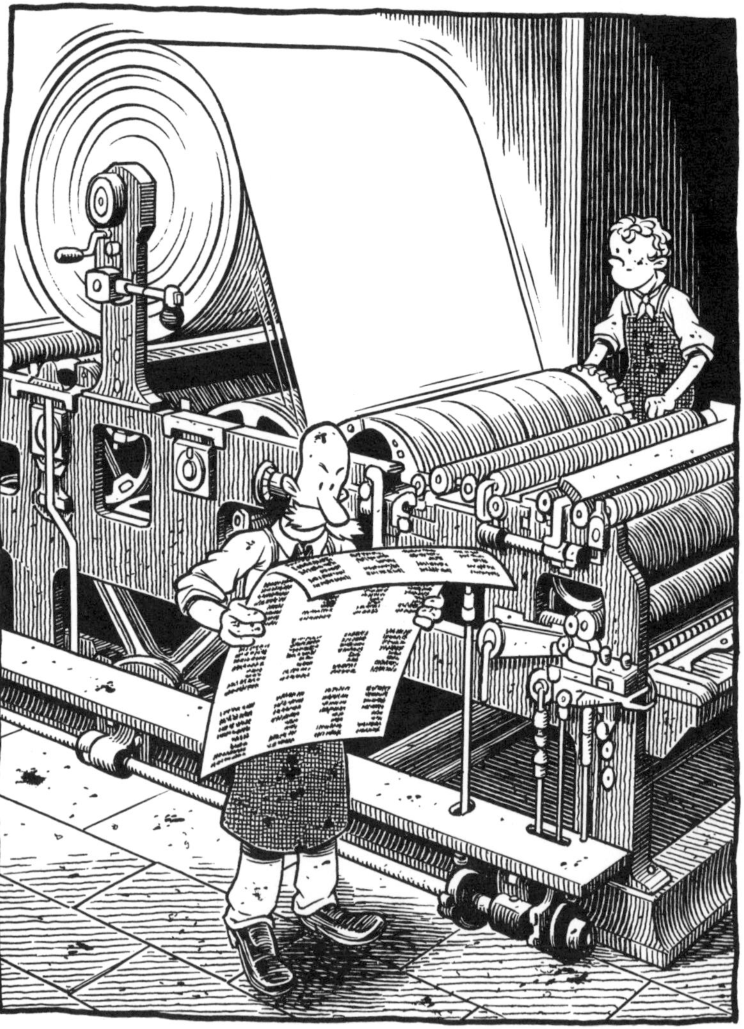

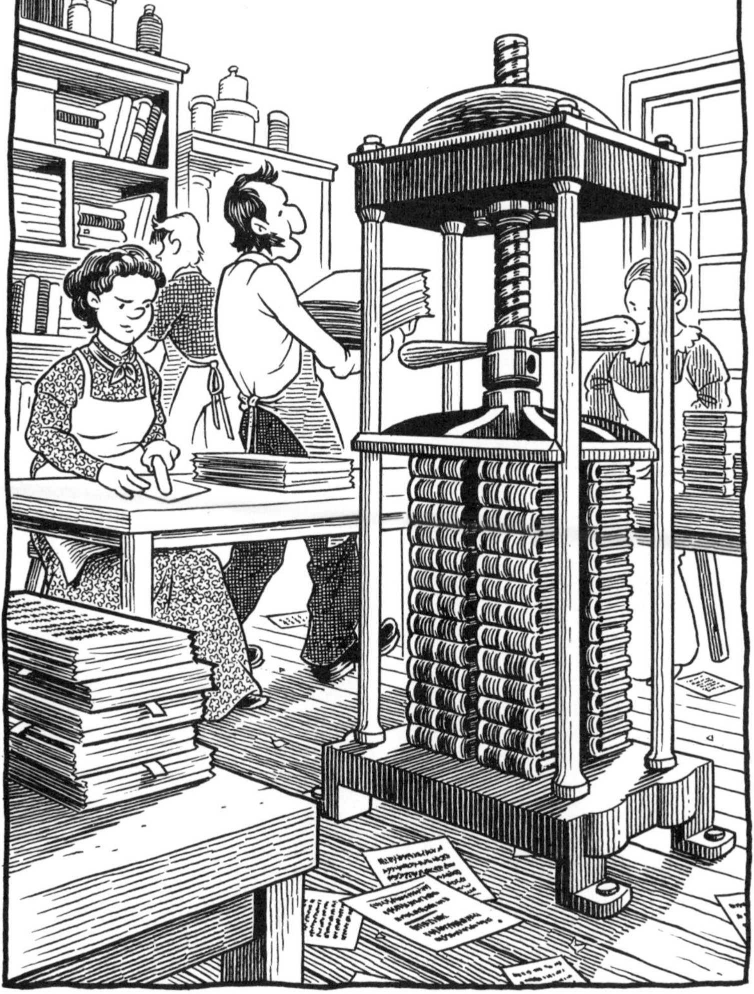

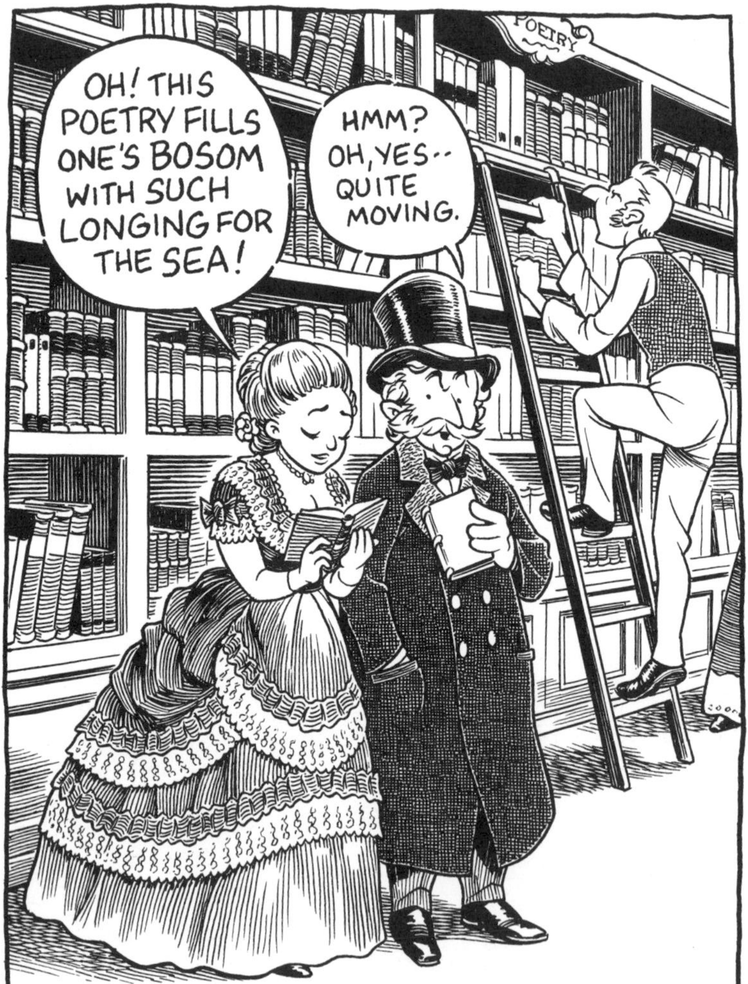

POETRY
OH! THIS POETRY FILLS ONE'S BOSOM WITH SUCH LONGING FOR THE SEA!
HMM? OH, YES.. QUITE MOVING.

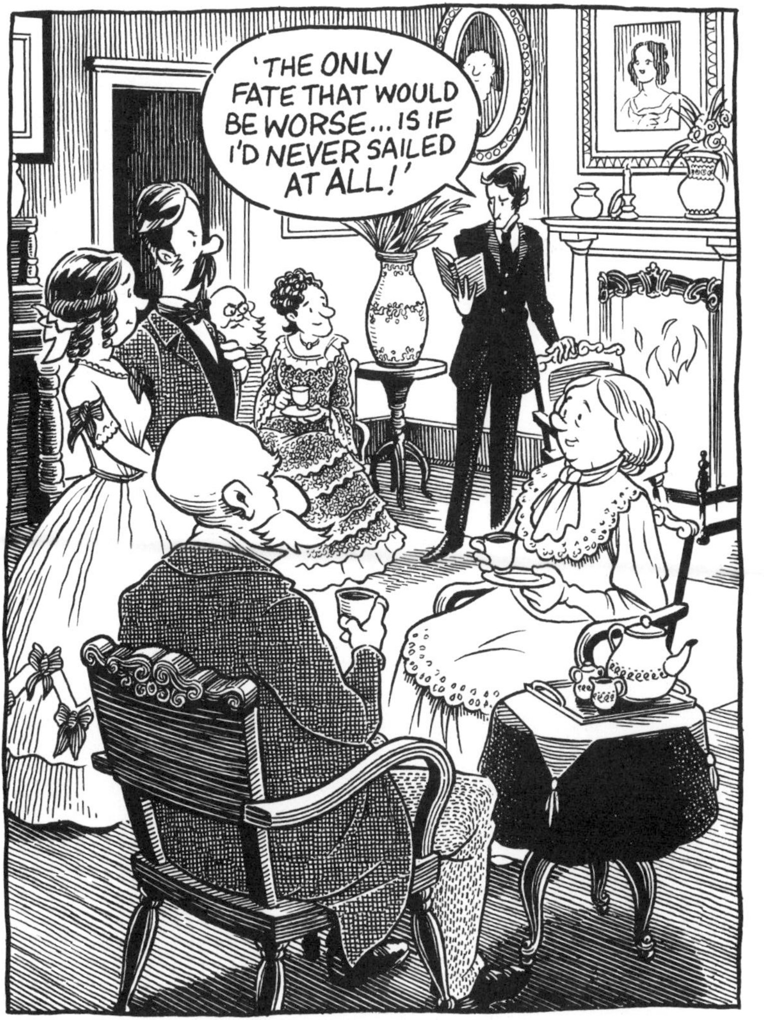
'THE ONLY FATE THAT WOULD BE WORSE... IS IF I'D NEVER SAILED AT ALL!'

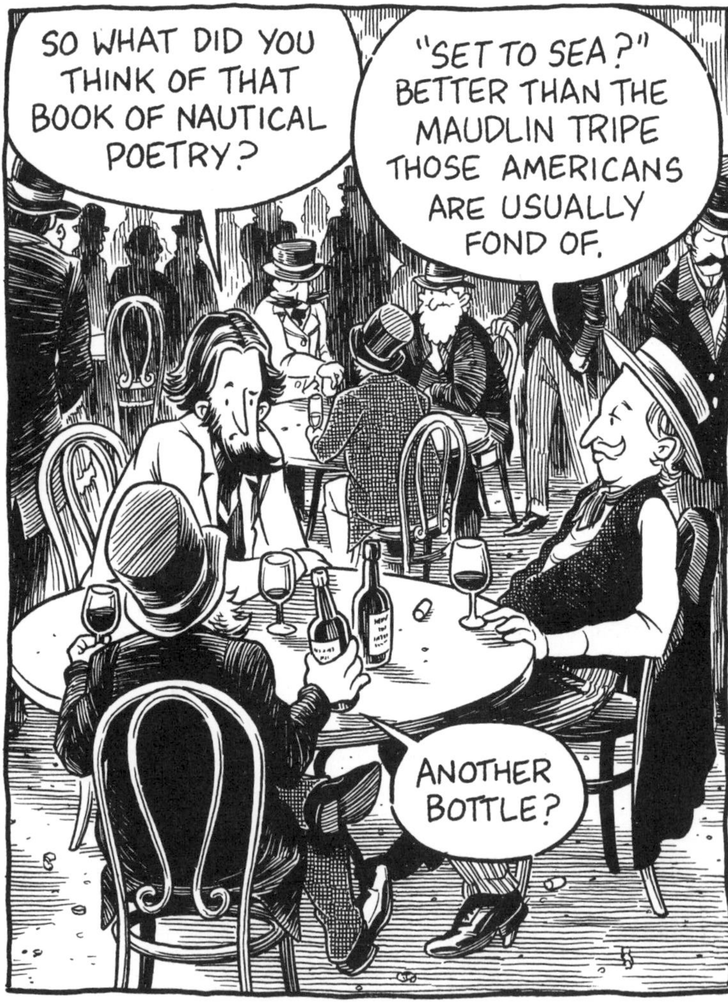
SO WHAT DID YOU THINK OF THAT BOOK OF NAUTICAL POETRY?
"SET TO SEA?" BETTER THAN THE MAUDLIN TRIPE THOSE AMERICANS ARE USUALLY FOND OF.
ANOTHER BOTTLE?

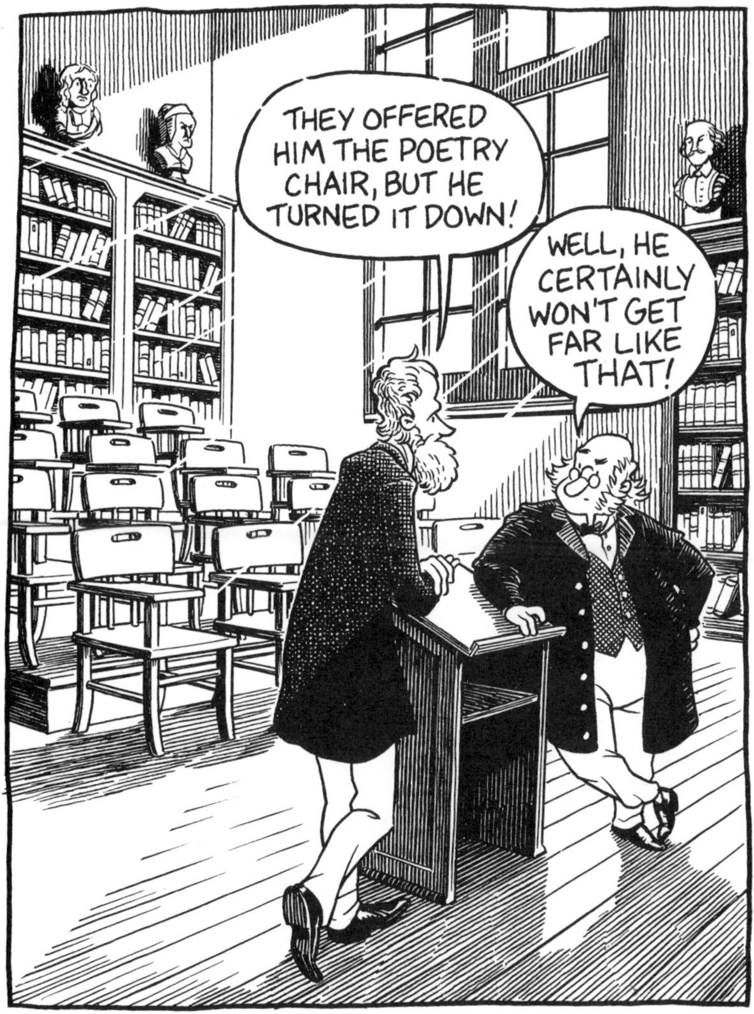
THEY OFFERED HIM THE POETRY CHAIR, BUT HE TURNED IT DOWN!
WELL, HE CERTAINLY WON'T GET FAR LIKE THAT!

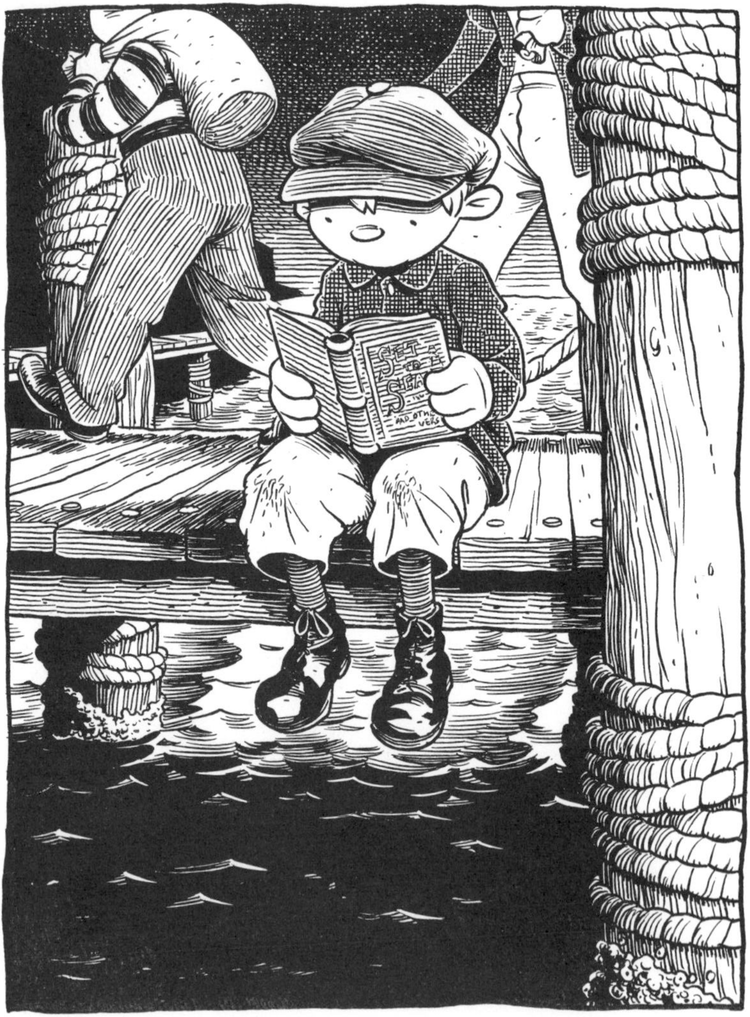

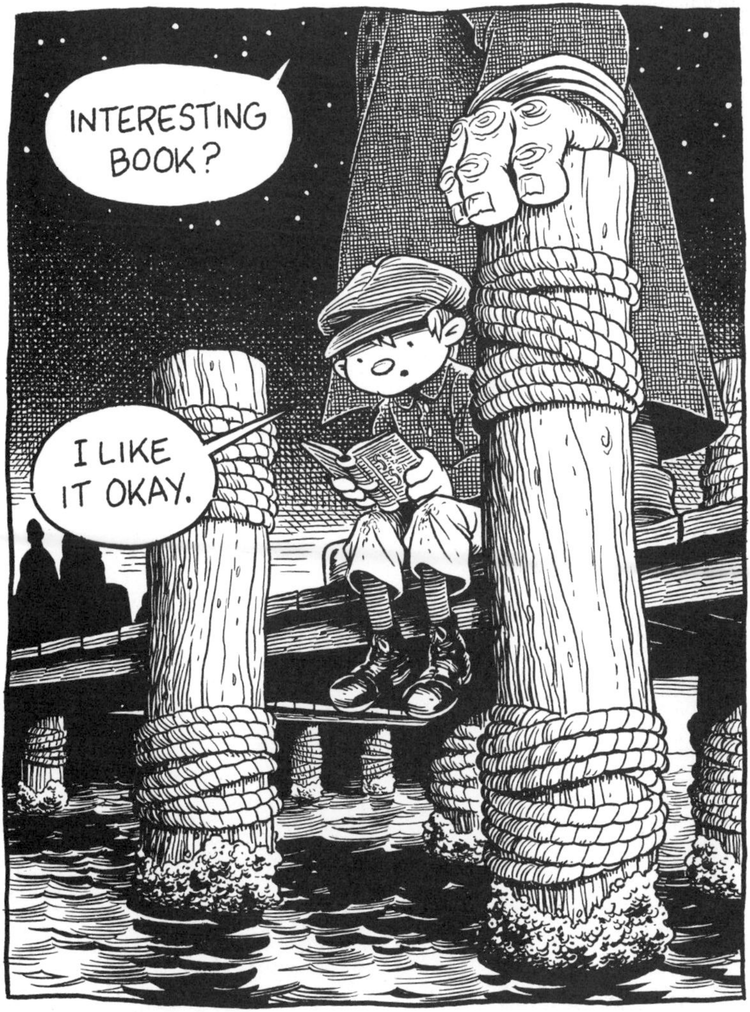
INTERESTING BOOK?
I LIKE IT OKAY.

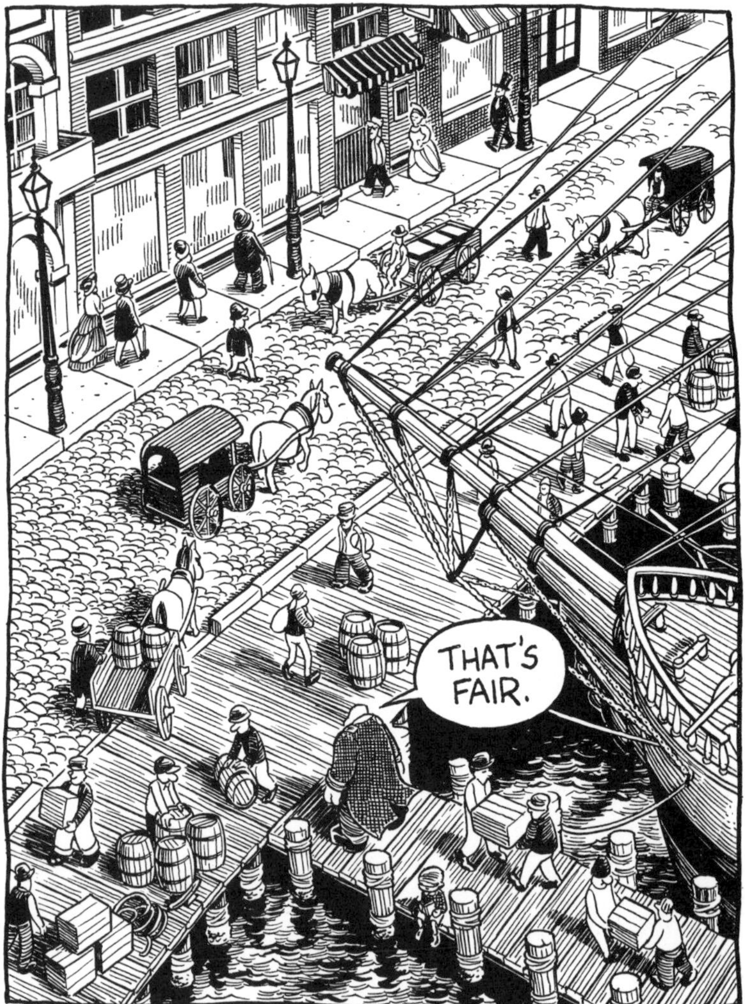
THAT'S FAIR.

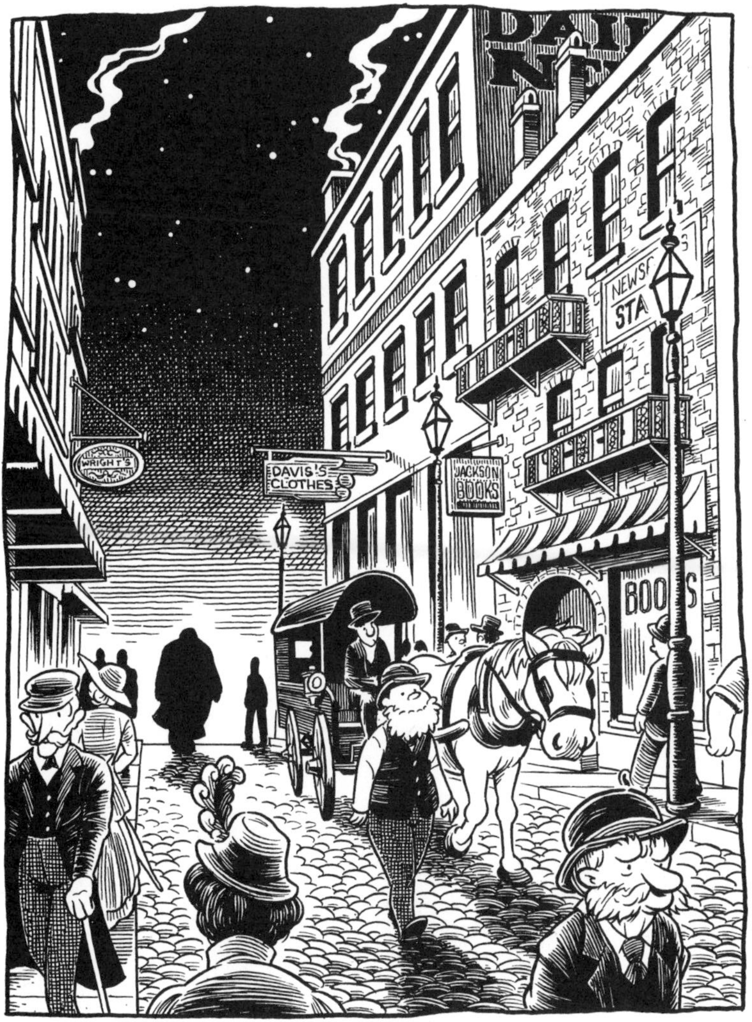
WRIGHT'S
DAVIS'S CLOTHES
JACKSON BOOKS

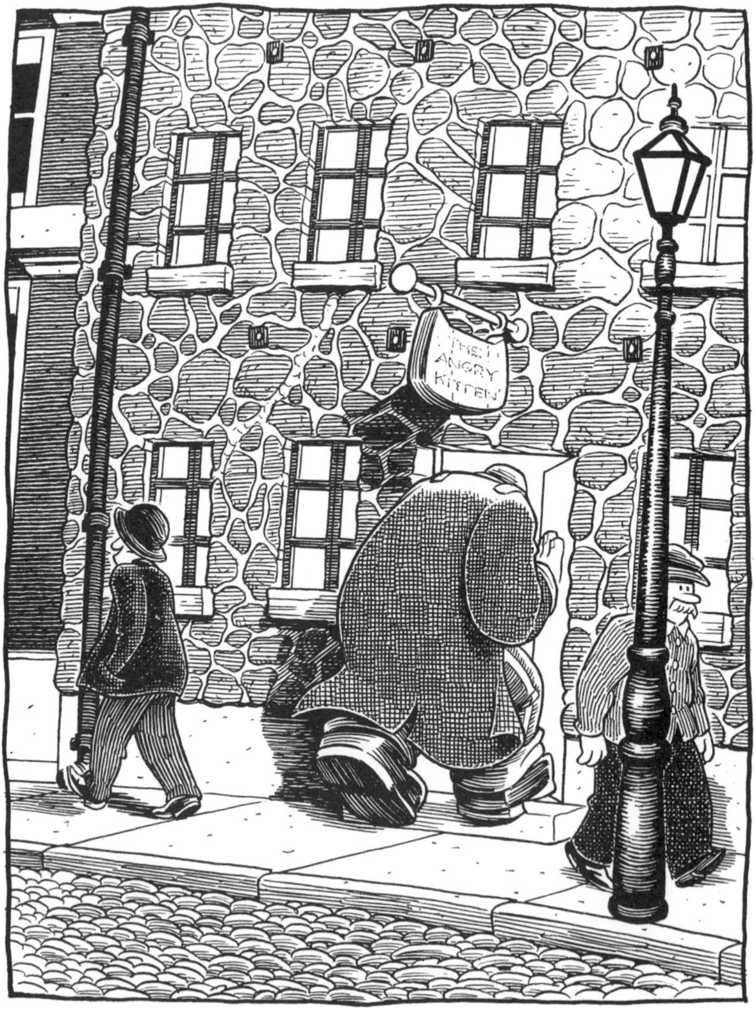
THE ANGRY KITTEN

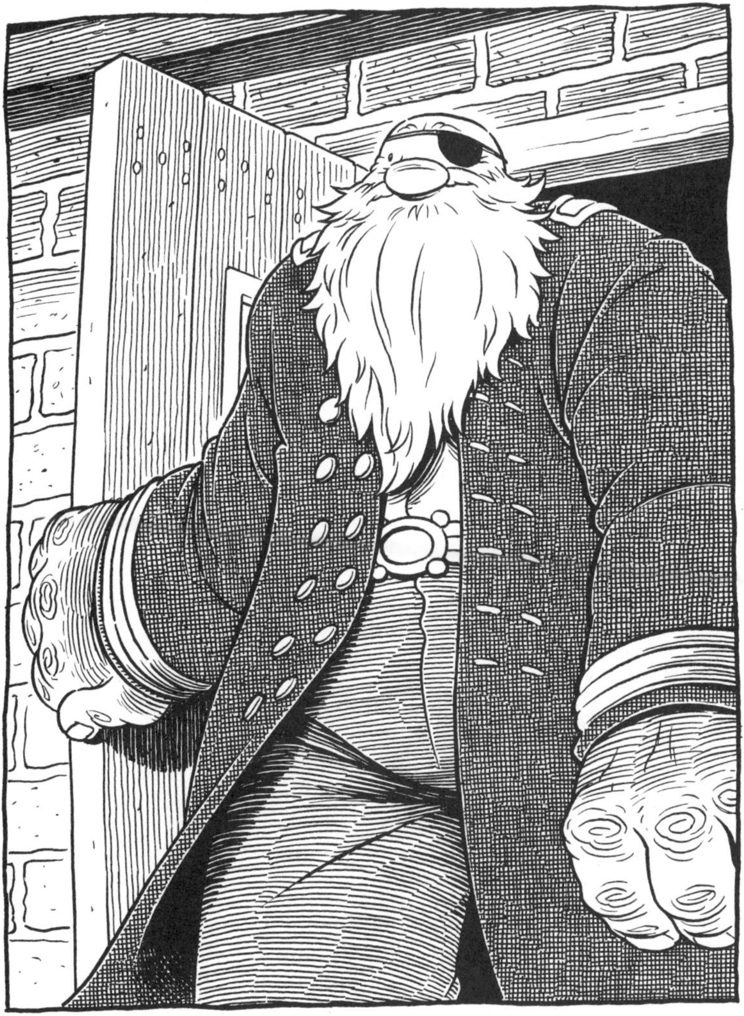

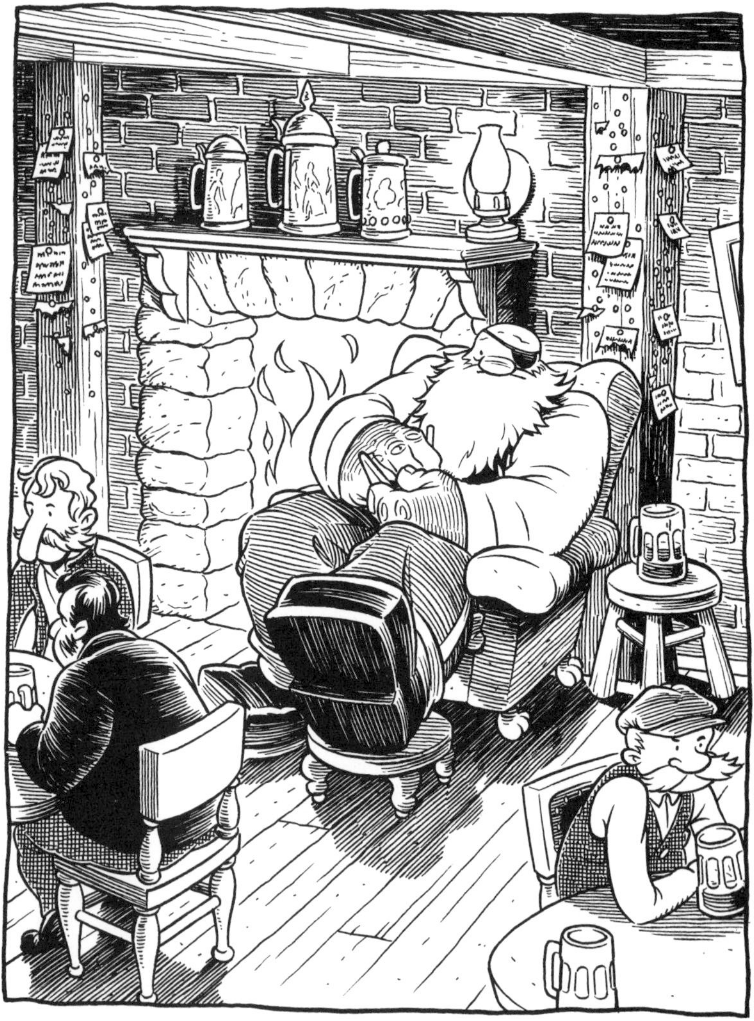

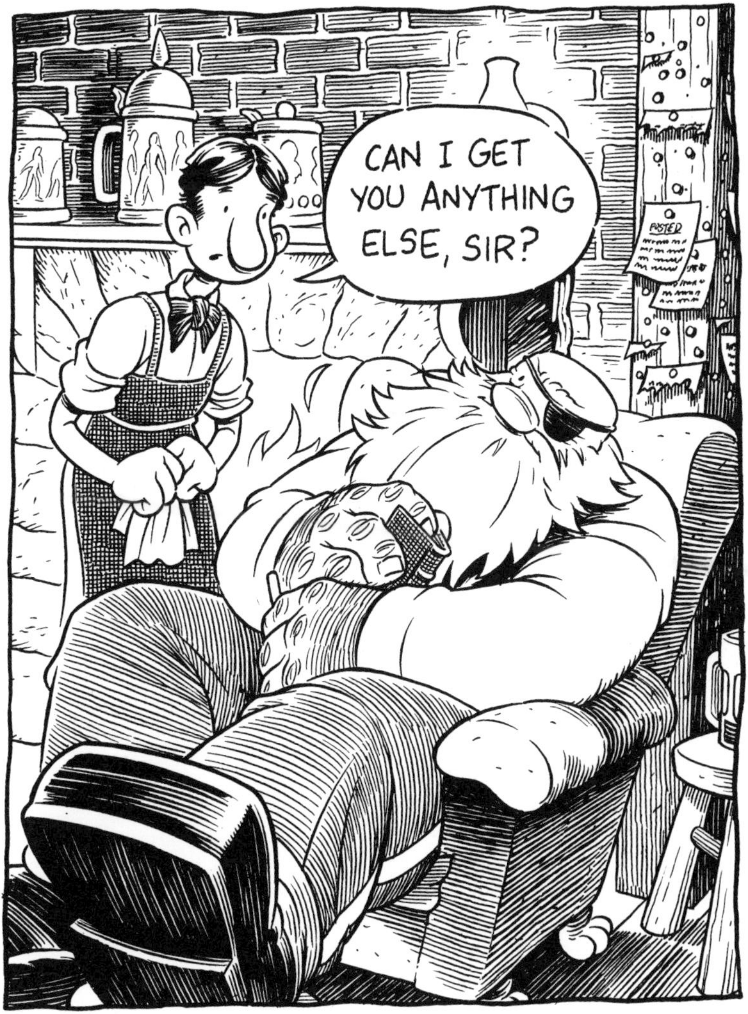
CAN I GET YOU ANYTHING ELSE, SIR?

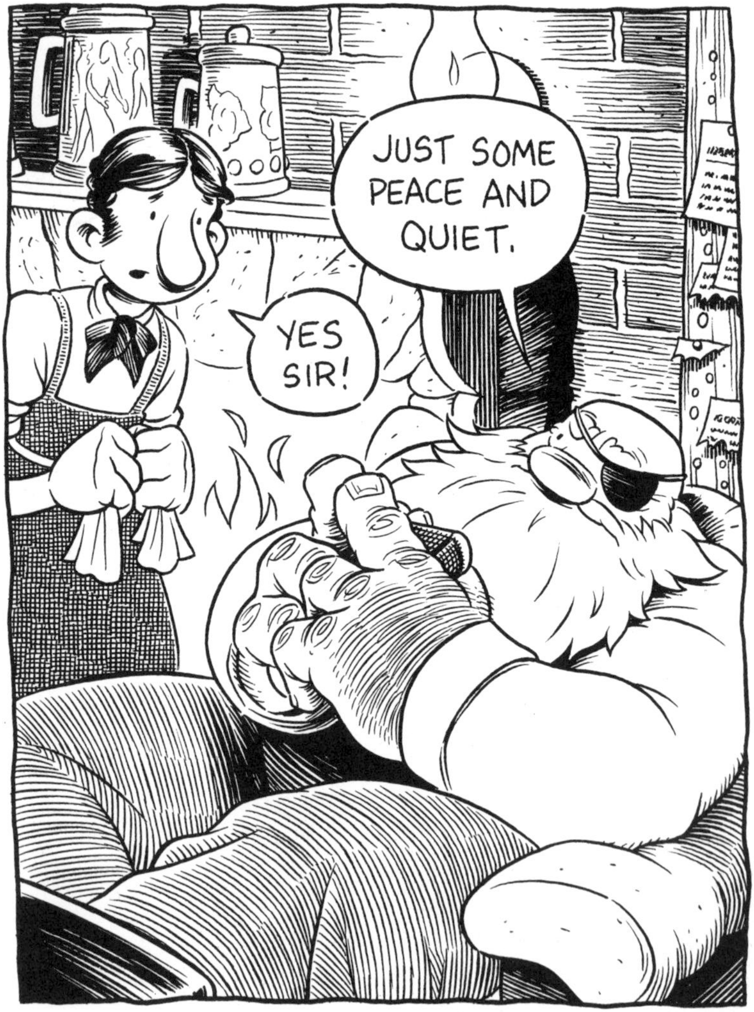
JUST SOME PEACE AND QUIET.
YES SIR!

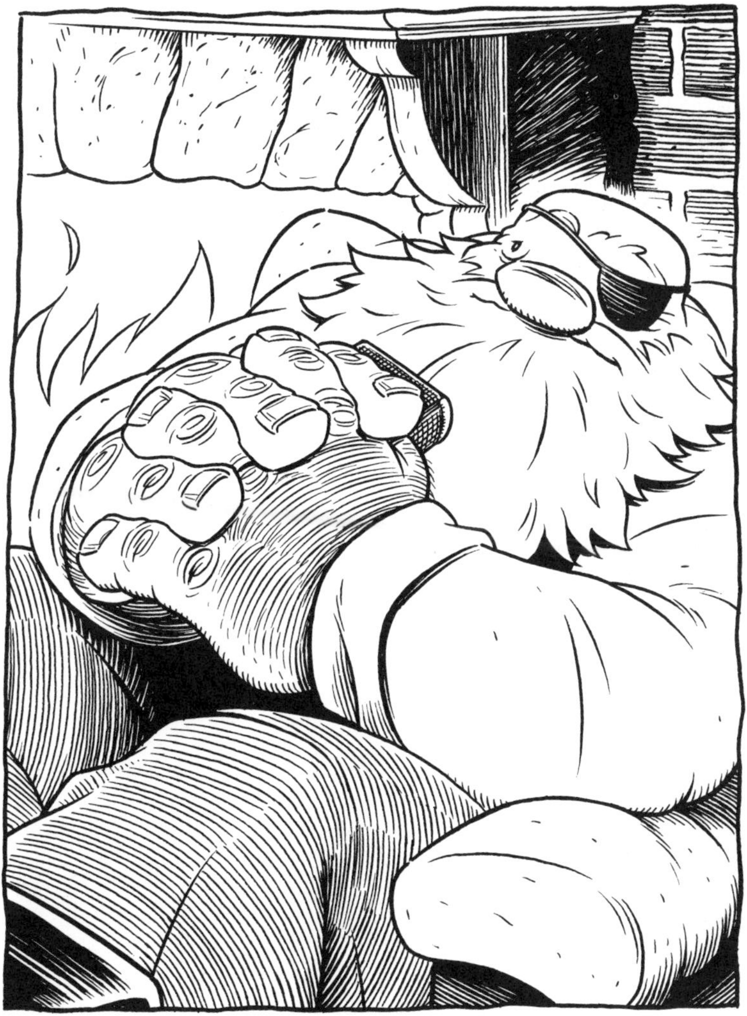

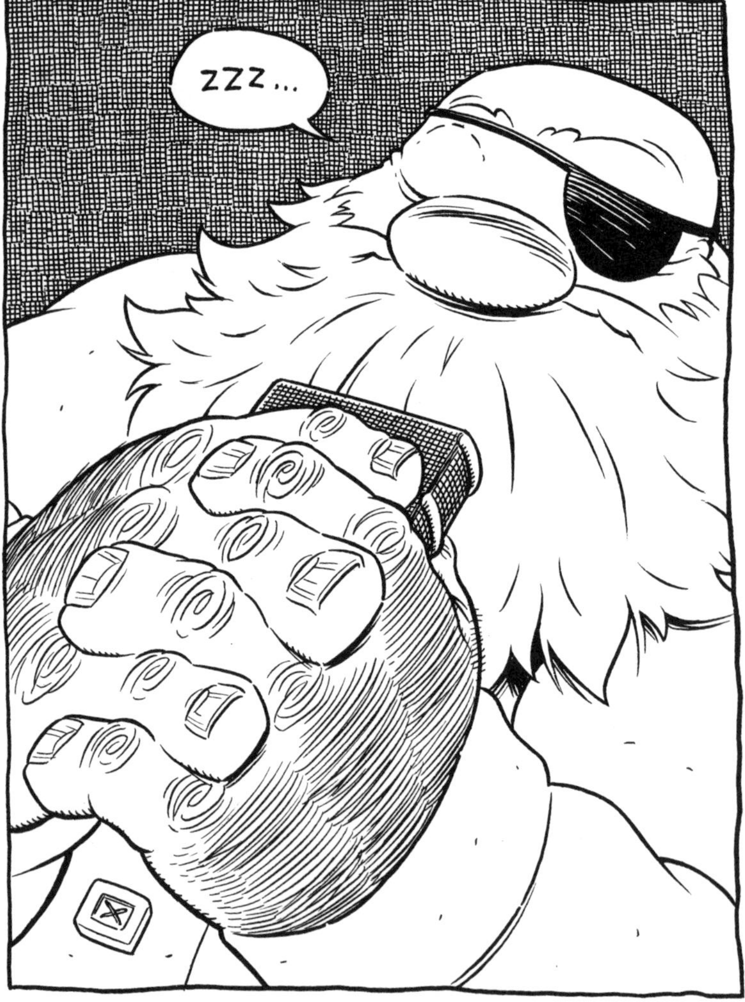
ZZZ...

Acknowledgments

Set to Sea owes a debt of inspiration to
the comics of my friend, Chris Wright.
Thank you to my mother, Lorene, and my
brother, Jeremy. Thanks to all of the friends
who gave me advice and support in the two
cities and five years it took me to get this
book together. And of course, infinite love
and gratitude to my wife, Eleanor.